Born 1977 in Belfast, Colin Murray is a national radio and TV presenter. He is the host of Radio 5 Live's *Fighting Talk* and hosts 5 Live Sport. In addition to this, Colin presents *Match of the Day 2* as well as a nightly highlights show on BBC2 during the World Cup.

A Random History of Football

COLIN MURRAY

An Orion paperback

First published in Great Britain in 2009
by Orion
This paperback edition published in 2010
by Orion Books Ltd,
Orion House, 5 Upper Saint Martin's Lane
London WC2H 9EA

An Hachette UK company

10 9 8 7 6 5 4 3 2 1

A CIP catalogue record for this book is
available from the British Library.

ISBN: 978-1-4091-0376-9

Typeset by Input Data Services Ltd, Bridgwater, Somerset

Printed and bound in Great Britain
by Clays Ltd, St Ives plc

Additional research: Joel Miller

The Orion Publishing Group's policy is to use papers
that are natural, renewable and recyclable, and made
from wood grown in sustainable forests. The logging and
manufacturing processes are expected to conform to
environmental regulations of the country of origin.

www.orionbooks.co.uk

Contents

4. Footballing Failures

5. The X Files

6. Breaking the Law

7. And When You're Not Playing Football?

8. What Could Have Been

***A to Z – one fact about every English Football League club and every
Premier League side in England, Scotland, Wales and Northern Ireland.***

(Centre) Forward

If one more person tells me that St Johnstone is the only British football league team with a J in its name, I swear, I'm going to stick my head in an oven.

And yes, I know that, of the current 92 English league clubs, there are 21 different endings, namely United, Villa, Athletic, City, Hotspur, Wanderers, Rovers, Albion, North End, Rangers, Palace, Wednesday, County, Argyle, Forest, Town, Dons, Orient, Alexandra, Stanley and Vale.

And no, you can't include Redbridge, because Redbridge isn't an ending, it's part of the place name, Dagenham & Redbridge.

This book will, I hope, breathe new life into your arsenal of pub trivia, through a random collection of lesser-known tales, collated from the history of the beautiful game. That's not to say that every fact will be a revelation, but my aim was to put together an assortment of stories that should offer up something new to even the most anal football fanatic.

The biggest problem was settling on a title. I eventually plumped for *A Random History of Football* because the subject matter pings around like some sort of literary pinball, never quite settling in one place long enough to become predictable. So much so that the chapter headings are almost surplus to requirements. After many hours of shuffling paper, I managed to section off the inseparable, but it's still amusingly tenuous at times.

Most football 'humour' books come in point form and are easily dispatched within a few quiet hours on the toilet. I've decided to pen stories, rather than lists, so I can confidently predict that *A Random History of Football* will transcend the shadow of Thomas Crapper's greatest invention.

One of the finest comedians in the world, Stewart Lee, recently launched a tirade on the 'toilet book': 'What does it tell us about our civilisation that the notion of the book is held in such low esteem that it is possible to append the word "book" to the word "toilet" and make the compound word "toilet book"?

'Library book, yes. Children's book, yes. Poetry book, yes. Toilet book, no. Toilet paper, yes. Toilet brush, yes. Toilet duck, you can have toilet duck. Toilet book, no.'

I'll always be a football fan more than a sports presenter, and I make no apologies for that. I can't, for the life of me, understand why some people would rather their commentators had no preferences or passion. That's the reason why Liverpool and Northern Ireland pop up more often than other sides because I follow both teams. However, I can confidently say that I've struck an unbiased balance, as is my job, highlighted most blatantly in one story in which I hail a Manchester United player as the greatest of all time. No, it's not George Best.

I'd also like to point out that, for better or for worse, every word written is by my own fair fingertips. As for research, I persuaded my mate Joel Miller, a real-life football statto, to help me out along the way. I'd like to thank him for his assistance and tolerance during the past months, when I would often call him in the middle of the night to ask essential questions such as, 'Is getting a monkey drunk actually against the law?'

I have also been making sneaky notes on a few interesting stories told by various esteemed panellists who appear regularly on BBC Radio Five Live's *Fighting Talk*, a show that I host on Saturday mornings between 11 a.m. and midday, so I doff my cap to them also.

Along the bottom of most pages you'll find an A to Z, which boasts one fact about every English league club, and every Premier League side in Wales, Scotland, England and Northern Ireland. While many of them are precious droplets of enlightenment, I struggled slightly when it came to the Welsh, due to the fact that many of the clubs are younger than I am.

Having finished the book, what's pleasing is that I have included almost all the original facts I wanted to, under various headings, with the exception of one, which I am now going to add here as a way of finishing this foreword.

When Christian Vieri signed for Inter Milan in 1999, the price of milk in the city rose, overnight, by a staggering 15 per cent. This was due to the fact that the Internazionale chairman, Sergio Cragnotti, was also the proprietor of the biggest milk company, and enforced the increase in order to cover the costs of the player's £31m transfer fee and his inflationary wage.

Therefore, every time an AC Milan supporter sat down to their cornflakes of a morning, they were actually subsidising the pay packet of their bitter rival's star striker.

Even in a book this random, I couldn't find any place for this little nugget.

I sincerely hope you enjoy *A Random History of Football*. I certainly had a ball writing it, even if it threatened to take over my very existence.

If enough of you buy it, then I'll once again cocoon myself indoors for three months, surrounded only by Red Bull, fags and microwave meals, and uncover *A Random History of Football, Volume II*.

1

Fights, Broken Bones and Sudden Death

1. The Referee's a ... Duck!

With the exception of Sir Alex Ferguson's anger-management counsellor, there's no more thankless job in football than that of a referee.

I, for the most part, sympathise with them. They're employing a dated system to marshal a modern game. Only nonsensical nostalgia and misplaced morals keep football officiating firmly stuck in the dark ages, while almost every other sport embraces technology to make the game more honest. There are some, I believe, who would happily return to jumpers for goalposts and pigs' bladders for footballs, if they had their way.

Personally, I would go as far as to say that some Premier League footballers disgrace the game far more than any misjudged sending-off or dodgy offside decision. That's why it always delights me when, on a rare occasion, a referee gains his revenge.

The most famous incident of this kind centred around

Aberdeen, the only Scottish club to have won two European trophies, effectively invented the dugout in the 1920s. Trainer Donald Colman didn't feel he could see enough from the Pittodrie grandstand, so he marked out an area on the touchline.

3

a player who, season after season, had been – and occasionally still is – a thorn in the side of officialdom. Robbie Savage holds the dubious distinction of being the most cautioned player in the history of the Premier League, contradicted by the fact that he's only been sent off once at club level, and a solitary time in a Wales shirt. He matches passion and talent with premeditated petulance and backchat, and rarely gives a referee a moment's rest. Even off the pitch he has terrorised the man in black, including one famous incident in which he used referee Graham Poll's toilet after being substituted due to, shall we say, bowel problems. The whole messy affair was dubbed 'Poogate' and Savage was charged by the FA for his porcelain-pressing antics.

Revenge came suddenly on an afternoon on Tyneside when referee Matt Messias, in full flight, swung out an arm, catching Savage full whack on his face, causing the bleach-blond brat to crumble in a heap, gaudily clutching his mug. To give Messias his credit, he immediately halted proceedings and leant down to check on his victim, although I would imagine, inside, he was overjoyed by such a random occurrence. He joined Dion Dublin (who once head-butted Savage) in carrying out an act that most football fans, in all honesty, had dreamt of doing. Adding to the amusement was Alan Shearer, who managed to pickpocket the referee, brandishing a red card to Messias and prompting guffaws and laughter from millions. Herein lies documentation of the only time in his entire life that Alan Shearer was funny.

Most people will remember this incident, partly due to its almost constant replaying on Sky Sports *Soccer AM* show, back in the halcyon days of Tim Lovejoy and Helen Chamberlain, so let me take you further into the less-known and, it has to be said, rather sinister history of the referee's revenge.

I assumed my research would uncover stories of fisticuffs and, possibly, serious injury, but I soon realised that referees have sometimes used more permanent methods to enforce their authority.

Prior to the beginning of the 2004 South African Premier Soccer League, 33 referees and officials were arrested on allegations of match-fixing, during a police sting codenamed, wait for it, Operation Dribble. Genius.

However, no lawful intervention could have prevented what happened just months later, when South African football endured one of its darkest hours. It happened during a friendly game in the Eastern Cape coastal town of Kenton on Sea, between two neighbouring townships, Young Tigers from Marcelle and Mighty Eleven, the home side.

Problems arose after the ref, Ncedisile Zakhe, awarded a penalty and dished out a yellow card to the offending player. Both sides began the mandatory push and shove, and soon fists were flying. The decision, however, most enraged the Young Tigers' coach, 41-year-old Michael

---

Aberystwyth Town was founded in 1847 by just one man. Arthur Hughes advertised in the local paper for players and staff, writing, 'Gentlemen wishing to join the above club are requested to attend a meeting to be held at the Belle Vue Hotel on Saturday, the 4th'. The rest is history.

Sizani, who, not contained by a technical area or fourth official, marched towards the referee to remonstrate.

Now, at this stage, with anarchy on the horizon, the ref had numerous options available to him. He could leave the pitch, refusing to carry on until order had been restored. Alternatively, he could resort to his notebook, booking players who had not yet gained control of their emotions. Possibly, given the blatant rule-breaking of said coach, he could send him from the touchline to a more removed position. Maybe, just maybe, he could have reasoned with the coach and explained the logic behind his penalty decision.

Ncedisile Zakhe did none of the above. Instead, he pulled out a 9mm pistol and shot Michael Sizani point blank in the chest. The bullet also struck the Marcelle manager and another player, although both survived. The Young Tigers boss, however, was not so lucky. He died where he lay. The murderer took to his heels, scaling a wall in an attempt to escape the law. Eventually, he was captured and sentenced to four years in prison.

Now, no matter how often Robbie Savage can annoy, I could not have condoned Matt Messias pulling out a Beretta and pumping the former Welsh international full of lead. Still, it would have been interesting to see whether Alan Shearer would have had the audacity to repeat his red card gag whilst staring down the barrel of a smoking gun.

Unfortunately, in South Africa this was not an isolated incident, as events on the football field reflected out-of-control gun crime in the country itself at the time.

I give you the Wallabies of Hartbeesfontein against

neighbour rivals the Try Agains in a game that took place in February 1999 in front of 600 spectators. This time, however, the episode is less cut and dried, and the referee in question did go on to plead innocence against the murder charge, claiming he had acted in self-defence.

The Wallabies were cruising at 2–0, before their opponents pulled one back in what were, shall we say, dubious circumstances. The ref awarded the goal, causing some fans to invade the pitch in protest. As things became hairy, referee Lebogang Petrus Mokgethi actually left the pitch to retrieve his 9mm pistol. He'd given it to a friend in the crowd to safeguard, which puts into context the backdrop against which this match was being played.

Wallabies captain Isaac Mkhwetha also had a touchline surprise up his sleeve, fetching a knife from his kit bag. As he lunged towards the referee, Mokgethi drew his weapon and shot the captain dead. He then promptly, and rather randomly, escaped on horseback, before being brought to heel by the authorities. He was released on $980 bail after pleading not guilty to all charges.

So, while we should not make light of these cases, it does make you wonder how much lip Wayne Rooney would dish out if he knew Steve Bennett had a semi-automatic tucked into his waistband. And would John

---

Accrington Stanley's rise to the Conference was made possible by a former player. They received £50,000 when Brett Ormerod moved to Blackpool, but it was a clever sell-on clause that earned them £250,000 when he progressed to Southampton.

Terry really stand up for his mate Frank if Andy D'Urso had a Smith & Wesson conveniently concealed around his groin area? Something tells me the life of referees would become instantly easier if they added the weapon to the whistle but, alas, I think we'll have to settle, eventually, for video replay.

2. Step away from the Ironing Board

Premier League footballers, almost to a man, are contractually obliged not to kick a football outside of official training, match days and international duty. As part of their lucrative deals, they must forfeit all other forms of footie, from the park kickabout to the midweek five-a-side at the local leisure centre. Technically, by the letter of the law, a back garden frolic with your two-year-old son would be in breach of contract.

If Man City is shelling out close to £100,000 a week for the services of Gareth Barry, it's understandable that they do not want to lose him to a bad slide tackle from Billy the bricklayer during a game of shirts and skins.

Clubs make every effort to protect their assets, which is why so much is invested in futuristic treatment facilities, special diets and watertight contracts that aim to limit the risk of injury to their star players. Some injuries, however,

AFC Bournemouth was fourth from bottom of the Football League when the team knocked FA Cup holders Manchester United out of the tournament in 1984. Their gaffer, Harry Redknapp, was just three months into his first managerial appointment.

you just can't predict. No contract in the world could possibly legislate for the inanimate object.

Most famously, goalkeeper Dave Beasant was sidelined for two and a half months while at Southampton in 1993 after a snack-fest went awry and he launched a bottle of salad cream towards his foot. But delve a little deeper and you'll find a labyrinth of dubiously obtained bumps, bruises, broken bones and pulled muscles.

Some say Spanish footballers need to spend more time worrying about the game and less time about metrosexual grooming, with one player in particular learning the hard way. Santiago Canizares, goalkeeper at Valencia at the time, missed the entire 2002 World Cup after carelessly dropping a bottle of aftershave on his foot, when shards of glass severed a tendon.

Serious injury can strike at the most unlikely moments, as Preston midfielder Simon Whaley can verify, with his midnight trip to the bathroom resulting in a marble top from his coffee table falling and crushing his big toe. Ouch.

From here on in it becomes quite absurd, a case in point being Norwegian international Svein Grondalen who, in the 70s, missed an international after disturbing a sleeping moose whilst out jogging. Not best pleased, the aroused animal chased the defender, who, fearing for his life, took evasive action by rolling down a hill, gashing his leg in the process. He needed stitches, whilst the people who learned of Moosegate were simply in stitches.

Closer to home, the award for Outstanding Contribution to Stupidity goes to Darius Vassell. Take a bow, Darius.

During his Villa days, the striker noticed a blood blister

under a toenail. Various options must have flashed through his mind. I assume he considered going to his local GP, showing it to his club doctor or, just maybe, leaving it alone. Instead, Darius decided the best idea was to drill a hole in his nail in order to relieve the pressure. Now, without wanting to cause offence, this sounds like the kind of action only Homer J. Simpson himself would undertake. The result, of course, was an unwanted hole and a dangerous infection that would sideline Vassell for weeks.

Rivalling him in the witless stakes is Rochdale's Lee Thorpe, who ruined his season after an ill-advised arm-wrestling battle on the team bus on the way to a vital play-off match with Darlington. The result? A broken arm ... in three places.

Another major threat to the average footballer is man's best friend. Various star names have been struck down by far-fetched injuries caused by their pooches.

Recently, Stoke's Liam Lawrence did his ankle as he stepped over his dog on the stairs, and if Spurs really want to get the best out of Carlo Cudicini, they need to have a word with him about his pet problems. He once suffered a knee injury after giving his dog, and I quote, 'a sharp tug' whilst out for a leisurely stroll.

Sometimes, the canine itself doesn't have to be directly

Airbus UK, formed by an aerospace company, has an unusual feature at their home ground, the Airfield. For safety reasons the floodlights have to be retractable, as the pitch stands adjacent to an active runway.

involved. Former Chelsea and Wales international Darren Barnard paid the price for not house training his dog, when he slipped in a puddle of wee in his kitchen, again causing serious knee damage. If only both men had had the calming influence of Jimmy Greaves, who announced himself as football's equivalent to Doctor Dolittle in the quarter-final of the 1962 World Cup in Chile.

During a battle against Brazil, a dog brought the game to a halt after straying on to the field of play. Many players made fools of themselves in an attempt to catch the mutt – a similar scene to that in *Rocky II* when an out-of-shape Balboa tried to corner a chicken. Eventually, Greavesey calmly sank to his knees and beckoned the dog into his loving arms. Some say that he barked a form of secret doggy language, although he would later go on to reveal that the pooch, once safe in his grasp, urinated all over his England shirt. This didn't bring good luck, however, as Brazil went on to win 3–1. Two-goal hero Garrincha was so impressed with the dog's peeing antics that he adopted it after the game.

You know what they say. Never work with animals . . . or kids.

Kevin Kyle, a Scottish striker of some ability, who played for both Sunderland and Coventry, endured maybe the most painful injury of them all, when his baby son knocked over a jug of piping hot water on to his lap, scalding his crown jewels. For my male readers, I'll give you a few seconds to stop cringing . . . Ready? I'll continue.

If all of the above mishaps seem hard to believe, they're rendered almost conventional when you take into account that Croatia's Milan Rapaic once spent time on the treatment table after poking himself in the eye with a boarding pass at an airport, or that French goalie Lionel Letizi suffered a back injury from picking up a Scrabble piece off the floor.

What is it with goalkeepers and their peculiar injuries?

Michael Stensgaard, one of Liverpool's lesser-known number 1s, actually ruined his entire career thanks to an ironing-board incident. In an effort to, well, put it away, he inexplicably felt a pull in his shoulder, which effectively resulted in the end of his career.

I'm not finished yet. Richard Wright is double jeopardy! He joined the keepers' list of shame when he fell over a sign whilst warming up in the goalmouth at Stamford Bridge. What did the sign say? 'Players Are Requested Not To Warm Up In Goal Mouth'. He also fell out of his loft of an afternoon, whilst allegedly elevating his scrapbooks to that safe place. He was still recovering from his leg injury sustained from 'sign-gate', and now his shoulder took the force of the fall, once again placing him on the sidelines for a considerable period of time.

So embarrassing are these incidents that most are kept hushed up, due to the inevitable red faces they cause.

One such disputed example centres around an admission made by Paul Gascoigne in his autobiography in which he suggests Bryan Robson's exit from the 1990

Aldershot Town's return to league football in 2008 came after a record-breaking season in the Conference National, when they won the division with a magical 101 points.

World Cup was caused not by the reported Achilles injury, but by a drunken prank. After the Holland draw, Gazza claims a somewhat sozzled Robbo tried to tip his bed over, but managed only to slip. Captain Marvel lost control and the bed landed squarely on his foot.

True or not, the result was arguably a favourable one, as his replacement, David Platt, made a stunning impact, with England going all the way to the semi-finals, and that infamous penalty shoot-out.

So, Real Madrid fans, next time you spot Cristiano Ronaldo out walking his *perro* (I think that's Spanish for dog) or popping into his local tapas bar for a quick snack, beware ... it could end in disaster.

3. Til Death Us Do Part ... Twice

If football fans put as much effort into personal relationships as they did into following their team, the divorce rate worldwide would be next to zero.

I've personally travelled thousands of miles in the name of my beloved side, had heart palpitations, endured dark moods that lasted for days and, on the odd occasion, kicked various household pets. Poor Ginger ... if Cantona hadn't scored in the FA Cup final in 1996, he'd still be purring. Eric, you murderer!

There's a long, long list of famous fans – the Scouser with the badges, the birdman of Colombia, the Frenchman with his cock – but for every famous follower, there are a million unsung heroes, who have endured unthinkable hardship in the name of the beautiful game.

One story in particular caught my eye, and it begins and ends in a sleepy English village in the north-west.

Congleton Town FC may be the dictionary definition

> **Arsenal** not only hold the record for most successive seasons in the top flight, but also have the highest average league finish throughout the twentieth century, at 8.5, beating Liverpool and Everton into second and third places respectively.

of part-time football. They have spent more than a century buzzing around a number of regional divisions in the Cheshire area, winning a few titles along the way. However, perhaps their greatest moment was reaching the dizzy heights of the FA Cup first round in 1989, in which they lost 2–0 away to Crewe Alexandra.

Despite never breaking out of the regional football cycle, the club has remained in business due to the steadfast support of the locals, who have turned up religiously to follow their local side. In fact, their ground itself holds 1,300, including a 200-capacity seated area. If you think that's posh, you might pass out when I inform you that said area is covered. Yes, that's right . . . covered.

In turn, Congleton Town are involved in various local schemes and charities, and have tried to contribute to the community where and when they can. Given this closely knit environment, you can imagine the immense sense of loss and bereavement when the club received a phone call on the eve of a match in 1993 informing them that their oldest and most devout supporter, Fred Cope, had passed away. The mood on match day was understandably sombre. Very few talked about the potential three points that presented themselves at three o'clock, but instead huddled in groups, paying homage to their greatest fan. They regaled each other with tales of the recently departed, and tried to figure out the best way in which to honour his outstanding, unparalleled contribution.

It just so happens that, in the same week, World Cup hero Bobby Moore had also gone to that great stadium in the sky, so it was decided that a minute's silence would be observed jointly for a country's hero and a local hero.

It was a bittersweet union between fan and footballer, separated in life by a touchline, but in death by nothing. Some say that the first thirty seconds of said silence was the quietest Congleton Town's little stadium had ever been, broken only by sounds of grieving, as the terraces remembered a man who'd been as much a part of this club as the pitch, the changing rooms, the goalmouths and the dugouts themselves.

Halfway through the silence, an inconsiderate latecomer arrived with a clatter at the turnstile, where he was greeted by an open-mouthed club official.

Unaware of the tragedy that had befallen the club, he enquired as to who the minute's silence was for. The ticket collector took a deep breath and, with the blood draining from his face, informed the man, 'It's for Bobby Moore . . . and you.'

Yes, that's right. After he had spent his life thanklessly following this non-league side from cowshed to cowshed, from barn to barn, Congleton Town FC had declared their greatest and oldest fan, Fred Cope, dead. Now that's gratitude for you. As he made his way to the same place in the terrace that he'd occupied for decades, some fainted, thinking his spirit had risen just in time for kick-off, whilst others just stared in disbelief.

Aston Villa versus Everton is the most played fixture in the history of England's top division, mainly because Villa have spent 98 campaigns at the top, beaten only by the Toffees on 105. As of summer 2009, Villa have the edge, with 71 league wins to Everton's 70.

Throughout football history, clubs have put fans through all sorts of torture, off the field and on it; from the last-gasp winner to ever increasing financial woes. In my mind, there is no doubt that the beautiful game takes years off real fans' lives, but in the case of Fred Cope, his team officially killed him off.

When he eventually did pass away several years later, another minute's silence was held, although it is said there were a few nervous glances towards the turnstile.

4. You're through to the Final ...
Have You Got Life Insurance?

In the 21st century, the football surgeon is God.

No longer does a cruciate ligament injury mean the abrupt end of a career, as various advances in surgical procedures mean that just about any pull or tear can be repaired or, at the very least, patched up for a few seasons. Roy Keane, Paul Gascoigne, Robert Pires, Alan Shearer and Ruud van Nistelrooy are just some players who will happily pay testimony to that.

Hamstrings are probably the biggest concern, with the likes of Michael Owen and, more recently, Fernando Torres, being dogged with recurring strains, each time reducing their speed by vital inches.

This is why managers and coaching staff wrap their players in cottonwool. A multi-million-pound investment can evaporate with one poorly timed comeback or over-exertive training session.

History shows that the road to player protection has been a slow one, with horror stories the catalyst for the

---

Ballymena United won the prestigious Irish Cup on their very first time of asking. So impressive was their 1929 triumph that the Irish Football Association gave them the trophy to keep for ever.

---

introduction of substitutes in the first place. It used to be
that an injury penalised the victim's side, as they'd be
forced to play on with one man fewer. In crucial games,
the injured player would sometimes be asked to stay on
the pitch, even with blood pouring down his face.

There's hardly a trophy more deserved in Liverpool's
illustrious history than the 1965 FA Cup, which was won
thanks to the superhuman effort of a player called Gerry
Byrne. In the opening minutes a crunching tackle broke
Byrne's collar bone, yet he stayed on the pitch not only
for the full 90 minutes, but for the following half an hour
of extra time. Far from being a passenger, he actually set
up Roger Hunt for the Reds opening goal.

When Keith Peacock, on 21 August 1965, ran on to the
pitch for Charlton Athletic as the first ever substitute, it
was as a result of Gerry Byrne's broken collar bone which,
while courageous and heroic, was not pleasant to watch.
Incidentally, almost a year later, the legendary Archie
Gemmill became the first tactical Scottish sub on 13
August 1966, when he was sent on for St Mirren during
a cup tie. By the way, that gives Jim Clunie the dubious
distinction of being the first substituted Scotsman, but
nobody remembers that.

As an aside, one substitute became two during the 1987
domestic season, which was not increased to the current
three until 1994, and even then the lawmakers were
dragged kicking and screaming. The third reserve was
introduced exclusively for replacing a goalkeeper, but by
the time the 1995 English Premier League season kicked
off, it applied to any active player.

Back to the crunching history of the FA Cup final

which, for some reason, attracts gruesome tales of battered and bloodied players, the most horrific of which centred around Manchester City goalkeeper Bert Trautmann in 1956.

With all to play for, the number 1 lunged at the feet of Birmingham City's Peter Murphy, saving the day for City, but taking a swift knee to the neck in the process.

If a player suffered a head injury like that today, the game would be immediately stopped and the club doctor would probably enter the field of play alongside the physio, but back then it was all about a splash of water, a sniff of smelling salts and a quick rub from the affectionately titled 'magic sponge'.

Trautmann played the remainder of the match with aplomb, making some top-drawer saves, but was inevitably unable to halt Birmingham's charge for the Cup, ending up on the losing end of a 3–1 scoreline.

Trautmann collected his loser's medal just like everyone else, before making the long journey home, as gutted as the next man. Over the next few days he complained of recurring headaches, eventually heading to the local hospital, where x-rays revealed that, in the fifth minute of the 1956 FA Cup final, Bert had broken his neck.

Elton John's uncle, Roy Dwight, scored after ten minutes of the 1959 final, but managed to become

> *Bangor*, which has won ten senior trophies since its formation in 1918, has announced its voluntary withdrawal from the Irish Premier League, due to serious financial problems. Best wishes and good luck to all involved.

disconnected from part of his leg before the half was over, after Luton Town's Brendon McNally went in hard. Roy's nephew would go on to pen the hit 'I'm Still Standing', which is something Roy wouldn't be doing again for quite some time. Still, he was at least comforted in the back of the ambulance by the knowledge that his goal was the difference between the teams at the final whistle.

In the 1960 final, a cracked left shin would be responsible for the remarkable success of Wigan Athletic many decades later.

Blackburn Rovers' Dave Whelan's top-flight career was effectively ended in that match by a crunching tackle from Wolves' Norman Deeley. Although he would go on to play for Crewe Alexandra, it was the £400 compensation he received following his shin smasher that funded his first venture, namely a toiletries stall in Wigan market. From there, he made the millions that helped lift Wigan, an unfashionable footie team in a rugby league town, to the dizzy heights of the Premier League.

The showpiece final continued to look more like an Accident and Emergency ward rather than a game of football. Only three years earlier another Manchester goalkeeper, this time United's Ray Wood, fractured a cheekbone after six minutes against Aston Villa. Not only did he return to the field in the 33rd minute, but he also played on the wing, before heading back between the sticks to see out the game, though his efforts landed him no more than a loser's medal, as his team went down 2–1.

Remarkably, the curse struck again in 1981 when Spurs' Graham Roberts must have felt he had entered a war rather than a football match. Already bleeding heavily as a result of an accidental collision with a Man City player, the defender made a valiant effort to clear his lines with a header, but in stooping low took the full force of a blow from his own team-mate Chris Houghton, who booted him squarely in the face. Knocked out cold and covered in blood, Robert was now missing two front teeth, yet he refused to be substituted. Even at half time, when the team doctor told him it was ridiculous to even consider continuing, he was having none of it. Instead, he popped two aspirins (!) and played right through normal time and extra time.

All of these stories make the bleeding images of Terry Butcher in 1989 and Paul Ince in 1997 seem small beer.

Thankfully, such horrors are confined to the past. Well, nearly all of them ... Ask any Glasgow Rangers fan for their all-time list of real hard men and Trinidad & Tobago international Marvin Andrews will undoubtedly appear as often as Graham Souness.

In 2005, during a game against Dundee, the centre-half ripped his anterior cruciate ligament, the same injury that caused the aforementioned stars at the beginning of this piece to go under the knife for career-saving surgery.

After the game, Big Marv was told of his bleak situation, but dismissed any notion of surgery, despite the fact that

---

Bangor City was almost duped by an impostor claiming to be an Italian football star in 2005. Alessandro Zarelli arrived at the Welsh club making various bogus claims, but was eventually revealed as a conman. He fled Bangor without paying his hotel bill.

he had just suffered one of the worst injuries in football. Boss Alex McLeish called on top surgeons and world-renowned doctors in an effort to talk some sense into him, but to no avail. Andrews insisted his faith would see him through and, faced with a mixture of bewilderment and disbelief from all involved, set about a recovery programme that involved gym work, physio and a whole lot of prayer.

Andrews claimed, 'I prayed to God, and He spoke. God is not deaf, God speaks. When I speak to Him, He replies. God told me not to have the operation.'

After three weeks, he informed McLeish that he felt well enough to return, which made the subsequent statement issued by Rangers truly one of a kind:

Marvin Andrews sustained cruciate ligament damage to his left knee in the game against Dundee on Sunday, March 13. It is the medical opinion that he requires an operation. Marvin fully understands the advice he has received, however, he has declared himself fit and wishes to continue training and playing.

So who was right? God or the surgeon? The correct answer is the big man upstairs. Andrews would go on to start the last five games in what was a close-run season. On the last day, courtesy of a Celtic defeat and their 1–0 win away to Hibernian, Glasgow Rangers won the league title. That night, Marvin brought a whole new meaning to the term 'a good old knees up'.

5. Seconds out ... Here's the Gaffer

Experts recommend that if you are seeking a happy and stress-free life, you do not become an inner-city school teacher, an air-traffic controller or a football manager.

I know this only too well, given the palpitations I suffered when leading Inter Milan to a domestic league and European Cup double, and that was only on my computer. An ITV news programme once strapped Dave Bassett and Sam Allardyce to heart monitors during games. The results, on both counts, were disturbing, to say the least. Some have tragically paid with their lives, while countless others have gone under the knife for heart bypass surgery as a result of the trauma caused by running a football team.

So, you could argue that, for the good of their own health, they should let off a bit of steam once in a while, just as long as they don't take it quite as far as football's most fearsome managers.

Barnet's financial situation is eased regularly by Arsenal. The Gunners reserve side uses Underhill Stadium as its home ground and, as part of the deal, Arsenal play Barnet in an annual friendly every pre-season.

Now, before you all start screaming Sir Alex Ferguson
at the page, his hairdryer antics look like something from
a Mills & Boon novel when compared to other examples
of gaffers gone crazy. Yes, he deserves bonus points for
splitting David Beckham's forehead open after kicking a
boot at him, but his dressing-room piledriver was allegedly
unintentional. Harry Redknapp, on the other hand, knew
exactly what he was doing when he hurled a plate of
sandwiches at the head of Don Hutchinson.

It came after West Ham drew 1–1 with Southampton
in 1995, when Mr Houdini's post-match fury spilled over
into violence. Harry justified his actions by claiming, 'He
just wound me up too much. There was a nice big plate
of sandwiches on the table and he had the lot on his
nut.'

While this little tête-à-tête eventually sorted itself out,
there was no way back for Grimsby Town manager Brian
Laws, who ended up in the High Court after blowing his
top.

His dark mood following a 3–2 away defeat to Luton
Town in 1996 simmered, boiled, then exploded in the
dressing room, finding its way straight into the face of
Italian Ivano Bonetti.

Laws, who felt that the midfielder had not given 100
per cent, showed his disgust by hurling a plate of chicken
wings at him. The continental culprit also didn't make
enough effort to move out of the way of the airborne
poultry, resulting in a broken cheekbone and undisclosed
damages. He'd leave Grimsby at the end of the season on
a free transfer, while Laws stayed until well into the
following season.

The 'sticks and stones' rule comes into play at this point, but one manager deserves an honourable mention for his verbals.

John Sitton allowed Channel 4's cameras to follow him at Leyton Orient during their turbulent 1994/95 season, the result of which would become one of the greatest sports documentaries of all time.

His infamous machine-gun swear words have gone down in history, with the usual upshot of his outbursts being him inviting players outside for a fight.

In one instance, he informed two of his squad that if they had a problem with him they could 'have a f***ing right sort out'. Not content with the handicap of taking on both of them, he told the duo that they 'could pair up if you like, and you can f***ing pick someone else to help ya ... and you can bring your f***ing dinner, because by the time I'm finished with ya you'll f***ing need it.' What this last bit meant, I am not entirely sure. Certainly, I can see that after a scrap you may be hungry, but I can't work out why you'd bring your dinner with you.

Thankfully, the players refused.

Sitton's short fuse went on to provide us with some of the most bewildering sporting TV moments, the best of

---

Barnsley, third in Division Two in 1914/15, was robbed of promotion thanks to a dodgy Football League ballot. Arsenal, who had just moved stadium, was awarded the place ahead of them amidst allegations of bribes and corruption. It would take another 82 years for Barnsley to make it to the top division.

which came when he sacked one of his players during the half-time team talk.

And not just any player, but one who had played more than 400 times for Orient. That didn't stop Sitton from telling him, 'You come and see me tomorrow, you've got a fortnight's notice.'

Sitton talked a good game, but unless you raise fists or hurl a platter of food, you are not really in the Premier League of managerial bad boys, the most unlikely member of which is Trevor Francis.

A great footballer, no doubt, but a manager who could have done with a little bit more self-discipline. After his Crystal Palace side conceded against Bradford in 2002, a sideways glance revealed that his substitute goalkeeper, Alex Kolinko, was enjoying a right old giggle from the comfort of the dugout.

Clever Trevor claimed to have reacted by cuffing his player around the ear, but Kolinko said that it was in his opinion a punch to the nose. The fearsome Francis's jab landed him with a double fine, from both his club and the Football Association.

Brawling bosses are never too hard to find, but it's much more interesting when the player fights back, as was the case when Cambridge manager John Beck became involved in a half-time altercation with his own player Steve Claridge. A few wayward comments and, before you could say 'foul play', the pair started laying into each other.

However, far from creating a rift between them, Claridge revealed in his autobiography that his boss was actually impressed by his pluckiness.

After losing the game, he turned to the rest of the squad and screamed, 'It's a shame you b*****ds didn't show the same passion he did at half time.'

As I draw a line under the cloud of violent football managers, I would deserve a good old-fashioned kicking if I didn't pay homage to Brian Clough, one of the craziest of them all.

He regularly showed signs of insanity through his words and his actions, exemplified by one particular story from Roy Keane's autobiography.

In the dying minutes of extra time in a 1991 third round FA Cup replay against Crystal Palace, the 19-year-old Keano underhit a back pass to his Nottingham Forest keeper, Mark Crossley, allowing John Salako to score an audacious 45-yard equaliser. When the young Republic of Ireland international trudged into the dressing room, Cloughie greeted him with a short, sharp punch to the face. As a bewildered Keane hit the deck, his boss calmly said, 'Don't pass the ball back to the goalkeeper.'

Similarly, he is rumoured to have once hung keeper Crossley on a dressing-room peg and punched him in the stomach, as a way of registering his disappointment at his performance.

Birmingham City was the first English club to fly the flag in Europe, reaching the semi-final of the 1956 Inter-Cities Fairs Cup. They drew 4–4 with the mighty Barcelona, but lost the reply 2–1. Not to be deterred, they became the first English club to reach a European final in 1960, only to fall foul of Barca yet again.

Brian Clough, it seems, was always considered and concise in his doling out of punishment, and the players seemed to accept it, although telling the Leeds United team that they had won titles under Don Revie by cheating did him no favours during his now well-documented 44 days in charge.

While there can be no excuse for violence, if I had the choice between heart surgery or releasing the tension by landing an occasional right hook on the chin of an ungrateful footballer, I know which one I would choose.

6. And as We Go to the Judge's Scorecards ...

Call me a sentimental old fool, but I miss the physical side of football.

Okay, I'll admit that knee-high sliding tackles are rightly a thing of the past, but do we really have to book or even send a player off just because of a little bit of argy-bargy?

I remember a summer afternoon in my teenage years when a 30-a-side free-for-all was abruptly halted when I spooned a 20-yard piledriver so high and wide that the ball ended up nestling in a nearby back garden.

The gentleman resident of said house refused point-blank to return the ball, only to be challenged to a fight by one of my friends, the prize being our vital piece of equipment. What followed was a five-minute, Queensberry rules slugfest between man and teenager, the result being a win on points for our guy and a triumphant return of the football. In the aftermath both pugilists shook hands, and the game continued, although there was a

---

Blackburn Rovers could do with sending their staff to evening classes. They've spelt the name of one of their own players wrong on two occasions, leaving their then star striker to line up against Hull in 2009 with 'Roque Satna Cruz' on his back. In 2007, 'David Betnley' suffered a similar fate.

collective gasp when another audacious effort clipped the top of the same man's fence, thankfully resting on our side, therefore avoiding Rumble in the Jungle II.

While dangerous tackles have been rightfully outlawed, it is with eyes dimmed with sadness that we say goodbye to the Saturday afternoon push and shove. No longer can a player show his disregard for an over-enthusiastic challenge by standing toe-to-toe with the perpetrator, even if it's only to glance heads for a split second. If you raise a fist, foot or head, it's a straight red and an early bath.

Back in the glory days, Derby County's Franny Lee was as capable a fighter as he was a footballer. His punch-up with Leeds hardman Norman Hunter ranking as the most famous of them all.

Despite an obvious reach disadvantage, Lee gave as good as he got, trading blow for blow with the big defender after a series of altercations had led to all-out war. The first strike was delivered by Hunter, promptly splitting Lee's lip, before a blur of shots resulted in them both being sent off – only for the feuding to flare up again as they both headed towards the tunnel.

A long time afterwards, when Franny Lee was chairman of Man City, he unexpectedly bumped into his old foe, but there was to be no rematch. Instead, they shook hands, with Lee joking, 'Come on Norman, let's finish it off in the boardroom!'

The past is littered with glorious wingdings, Keegan versus Bremner in the 1974 Charity Shield being a particular classic.

The Battle of Santiago also ranks up there with the best of them, as Chile and Italy turned the 1962 World Cup into a police matter. The match was not broadcast live in the UK, but David Coleman introduced the highlights by stating, 'The game you are about to see is the most stupid, appalling, disgusting and disgraceful exhibition of football, possibly in the history of the game.' There followed punches, kicks, horror tackles, broken noses and police intervention. The referee was England's Ken Aston, whose experience that day, as you'll discover later in the book, no doubt inspired his most noted invention.

Lesser known is the tale of Barcelona versus Athletic Bilbao in the 1984 Spanish Cup final, which was only ever going to go one way, due to the following reason. Diego Maradona was returning from a broken ankle, caused by the Butcher of Bilbao himself, Andoni Goikoetxea. Andy to his team-mates.

The pre-match hype was more about revenge than silverware and, sure enough, after being goaded by certain Bilbao players, Maradona lashed out, setting off an 11-a-side brawl, which would have looked more at home in the Wild West than on a football pitch. It was a dust-up fit for a king, quite literally, as watching from the stands was none other than King Juan Carlos himself. Bilbao, blood stains on shirts, lifted the trophy, while Maradona trudged off, never to play for Barcelona again.

Blackpool's 1953 FA Cup final was named after Stanley Matthews, who inspired the team to glory after two previous losses in the finals in 1948 and 1951. However, it was Stan Mortensen who scored a hat-trick in that game, the only player ever to do so in an FA Cup final.

I assumed such ferocious encounters were a thing of the past, but it just requires a little bit more dedication to find them today and, thanks to our friends at YouTube, match-day dust-ups can be savoured over and over again.

Personally, I had no reason to tune into the second leg of a 2005 World Cup play-off between Turkey and Switzerland, but those who did were treated to much more than goalmouth action. Turkey went into the game two goals down from the away leg, and a 4–2 win in Istanbul was not enough thanks to the away-goal rule. The deflated Turks were less than pleased with the post-match Swiss celebrations and, from seemingly nothing, a tunnel war broke out involving not only the squad but the coaching staff, culminating in Swiss player Stephane Grichting being kicked so hard that he spent the night in hospital courtesy of a – quickly, cross your legs – perforated urinary canal. It was alleged that the offending boot belonged to none other than ex-Villa defender Alpay, although no blame was ever officially bestowed.

Sadly, all-out scraps during competitive British games are all but extinct, so thank goodness for 'friendly' matches!

QPR were the unlikely stars of a return to old ways when they welcomed China's touring Under-23 Olympic side in 2007, for a leisurely kickabout at the club's training ground. What took place has now been watched by more people worldwide than any other moment in QPR's history, thanks to a battle that saw Zheng Tao actually knocked out cold and the match abandoned.

QPR's assistant manager weighed in, and was arrested on suspicion of ABH, although I'm not sure the British prison system could have handled the influx of new felons had the police collared everyone who threw a successful punch or karate kick during the ingeniously titled 'Great Brawl of China'.

Nowadays, the price of waging war on the field of play is just too great, but inventive footballers have worked out how to get around this ... by battering their own players. Look closely and you'll see we are currently in the midst of an epidemic of friendly fire. Spurred on by the infamous Batty/Le Saux incident, and various fights involving Keith Gillespie, the last couple of years have given rise to inter-team boxing bouts ... and it's not just Joey Barton's fault.

Craig Bellamy, in 2007, stopped just short of thwacking his team-mate John Arne Riise with a golf club, rumoured to be a three wood.

What did the Norwegian defender do to deserve such treatment? He refused to follow Bellamy on to the stage during a night out at karaoke. Both players were sold by Rafa Benitez in the following months.

In 2008 we were spoilt for choice, but my favourite short, sharp strike came from then Arsenal player Emmanuel Adebayor and was aimed squarely at his hapless strike partner Nicklas Bendtner. The Gooners were losing 5–1 to Tottenham, and Bendtner was having a nightmare, putting the ball into his own net and

---

Bolton Wanderers' quest to win their first top league title has lasted longer than any other team in England. The 2008/09 season marked their 70th unsuccessful attempt, although they have lifted the FA Cup on four occasions.

generally performing as if he'd never seen a football before.

To add insult to injury, Adebayor head-butted him. Take note, Mr Tevez.

Ricardo Fuller also stands out from the list, after he railed against the concept of 'goodwill to all men', when he saw red for slapping fellow Stoke City professional Andy Griffin during a Christmas clash with West Ham in 2008. At the time, Griffin was club captain!

It seems fighting your own players is the safest way forward these days. When El-Hadji Diouf, a delightful man of beautiful manners, went toe-to-toe with Anton Ferdinand – strangely, after winning 1–0 against Fulham – the in-house wrangling reached new lows as Diouf threatened to stab his team-mate. Within days, the Senegalese striker was dispatched to pastures new.

Knives and golf clubs aside, I'm glad we've found time in this book to pay tribute to the rare breed of the foot-bawler.

7. Putting the 'Brat' into Celebration

When fantasising about scoring the winning goal in the Cup final, there are only two main considerations: how to score it and how to celebrate it.

Do you go for the Alan Shearer salute? The Robbie Keane roll? The Crouchy robot? Or what about Bebeto's rock-the-cradle? Personally, I'd opt for the Jurgen Klinsmann splish-splash.

The moments immediately following a successful strike are precious to a footballer. They represent guaranteed face-time. Every television camera, every flash bulb, every fan, is focused on you, and you alone. It's this knowledge that causes players to do the most ridiculous things, from shadow boxing corner flags to converting a triple somersault with half pike. With such a blank canvas to express themselves on, it's not surprising that things don't always go according to plan.

The most famous example is Steve Morrow, who scored

Bradford City's financial worries have been eased thanks to the unlikely figure of Harry Potter. The character's house scarf at Hogwarts School is almost identical to the club's scarf, causing wannabe wizards to snap them up in their thousands.

his first ever goal for Arsenal in the League Cup final, 1993, against Sheffield Wednesday. Not just any goal, but the winning goal.

After the game, caught up in the glory, captain Tony Adams attempted to hoist Morrow into the air, only for the Ulster man to fall awkwardly and break his arm. Instead of collecting his winner's medal, he received oxygen and was rushed directly to hospital. In a double blow, the injury kept him out of the FA Cup final, just a month later.

Ole Gunnar Solskjaer's 1999 Champions League final winner also came at a heavy price. His sliding celebration ripped his medial ligament and ruled him out for quite some time.

The line between ecstasy and agony is a fine one, especially when the adrenalin rush of scoring attacks a player's senses. Sometimes, you don't even have to be the scorer to get carried away in the afterglow.

Paulo Diogo set up a goal for Swiss side Servette against Schaffhausen in 2004, and celebrated with his team-mates. He rushed to the side of the pitch and jumped on to the perimeter fencing that separated the players from the fans. Unknown to him, his wedding ring had got caught on the railing, so when he leapt back to earth, his finger stayed right were it was. Efforts to reattach it were unsuccessful, although Diogo remained fairly pragmatic: 'I'm not dead and life goes on. So I have to live with one less finger.'

At least Argentinian striker Martin Palermo scored the goal that brought about his downfall, quite literally. After bagging one for Villa Real against Levante in 2001, he jumped on to a concrete wall, but when some fans joined him, the structure collapsed beneath their combined weight, leaving him with a broken leg.

You can't really blame him for over-reacting, given that, playing for his national team, he once missed three penalties in one game against Colombia in the 1999 Copa America.

While it's easy to feel sympathy for all of the above, I find it hard to show even a drop for the legion of players who risk their career by pulling off a gymnastic move after slotting home. When Celestine Babayaro joined Chelsea in 1997, he immediately somersaulted his way to a damaged ankle after scoring in a pre-season friendly, delaying his competitive debut until October.

While most ill-fated circus acts are well intended, some use the celebration as a way to address issues outside of football.

In 2005, while playing for Lazio, Paolo Di Canio ran triumphantly to his adoring fans and offered a raised-arm salute that sent shockwaves through the game. Faced with charges of anti-Semitism, he stated, 'I am a fascist, not a racist.' Thanks for clearing that one up for us, Paolo! This didn't stop the Italian football authorities from fining and banning him for one match.

It's sound advice to stay clear of celebration statements,

Brentford boasts a list of celebrity fans to put any Premier League club to shame, thanks to a famous Hollywood restaurateur called Dan Tana. His passion for the club has rubbed off on megastars like Cameron Diaz and Jim Carey.

especially when it involves the Old Firm. Paul Gascoigne played an invisible flute after scoring for Rangers against Steaua Bucharest in 1995. This reference to Orange marching bands caused such an uproar that Gazza apologised for the gesture, claiming that his team-mates had told him to do it and he had no idea what it meant. He also promised never to do it again, but repeated the trick whilst warming up as a substitute three seasons later, only this time the opponents were Celtic.

It seems some footballers just can't resist abusing their moment of glory. It cost defender David Norris £5,000 plus two weeks' wages. His former Plymouth team-mate Luke McCormick had been jailed for over seven years after tragically, and drunkenly, crashing his car into two youths, causing their deaths. After scoring for Ipswich against Blackpool in 2008, Norris made a handcuffs sign as a show of support for McCormick.

Most commonly, however, footballers use their face-time as a way to hit back at fans who've been giving them stick, like Steven Gerrard did at Old Trafford when he scored a penalty against Manchester United in his side's unexpected 4–1 demolition of their arch rivals. His badge and camera kisses were a reaction to a chant opposition supporters directed at the Liverpool captain, with the line, 'he kisses the badge on his chest, then hands in a transfer request'.

Robbie Fowler did a similar thing after Everton supporters sang songs accusing him of being a druggie. After pretending to sniff a white line, a direct reference to cocaine, he was slapped with a four-match ban. Not funny, although then manager Gerard Houllier's defence of his player was downright hilarious. The Frenchman claimed that Fowler was pretending to eat the grass, replicating a popular African football celebration that Rigobert Song had taught him in training.

Others, however, couldn't possibly wriggle their way out of trouble. Lee Trundle starred in Swansea's Millennium Stadium Football League Trophy win against Carlisle in 2006, but after the match the striker unveiled a T-shirt of a cartoon Swansea player urinating on a Cardiff City jersey.

Just in case his point hadn't been made, he then held up a Welsh flag with the immortal words 'F**k off Cardiff' emblazoned on it, although it didn't have any asterisks in it. As a result, Trundle was arrested, along with fellow team-mate Alan Tate, on suspicion of public order offences.

To my knowledge, however, only one player has ever used the scoring of a goal to blast his own fans. After putting the ball in his own net for Arsenal against Coventry at Highbury in 1979, full-back Sammy Nelson was hit with a torrent of abuse from the home support. His reaction? Well, he dropped his pants and mooned them! That'll be a £750 fine and a two-game suspension, thank you very much.

Brighton and Hove Albion was £9.5m in debt in 2004, so squad members helped to raise cash for the club by posing nude for Christmas cards, although the majority of the money was eventually raised via the pockets of their directors, rather than the lunch boxes of the players.

Finally, the opposite end of the scale came in 1974 when ex-Manchester United player Denis Law scored for Manchester City against his old club. Not only did it seal the win, but it condemned his beloved Red Devils to relegation. He has since admitted that he didn't even want to start the game, and felt physically sick after scoring.

I think the next time I fantasise about scoring for Northern Ireland at Windsor Park, I might just go for the straightforward fist in the air and jog back to the centre circle. It's safer that way.

2

Start the Fans ... Please!

8. 1 Across – Is This Pen Permanent? (5 letters, anag.)

No true football fan should ever change allegiance, regardless of owners, results or league position.

There's nothing more annoying than the disloyal dumb-ass who throws out his Chelsea top for a Manchester United one, only to replace that with the Arsenal away kit just 12 months later.

Thankfully, these part-timers are few and far between, with the majority of followers signing up for life; a timeless vow of love, devotion and (blind) faith, for better or, more likely, for worse.

There are many ways to show your commitment to the cause. You can travel thousands of miles, buy season tickets, join fan clubs; but all of these options can expire, leaving only one foolproof way to honour your beloved club permanently. The tattoo has long been the preferred demonstration of undying love, and football is no exception.

Bristol City became the first ever English side to suffer three consecutive relegations in the early 1980s. They only survived extinction after eight senior players all agreed to leave the club for just half the money remaining on their contract.

The common choice is a straightforward club badge or crest, usually on the forearm or over the heart, but it's important to take time to consider your decision, as it's more painful to remove body art than it is to have it scraped into your skin in the first place. If well thought out, it can prove a constant source of enjoyment, as I've found myself. On my left wrist, I have five red stars tattooed in a line, leaving room, I hope, for a few more over the coming decades. I went under the needle to commemorate my team's fifth European Cup success, a match I was lucky enough to witness first hand, along with ten friends, in Istanbul.

Now, every time I catch sight of the tattoo, it reminds me of an amazing week and the greatest game of football I am ever likely to witness.

While I have no regrets, other fans have dashed for the ink and lived to rue the day. Just recently, a 25-year-old Manchester City fan was so overwhelmed with the news of Kaka's arrival at Eastlands that he threw on his coat and headed straight to the city centre, demanding to have the name of his new hero tattooed across his chest.

Fast-forward a week and Kaka had turned down the mega-deal, opting instead to stay at AC Milan and, in doing so, leaving Chris Atkinson with a sore chest and a red face. He told the *Manchester Evening News*, 'Kaka's one of my favourite players. I got carried away by the emotion of him coming here.'

That you did, buddy.

Still, he's not opting for laser removal just yet. 'I just hope we go for him this summer.'

Congratulations, Chris, you are now the proud owner of a Real Madrid tattoo.

This goes to show that rule number one of football tattoos is to wait until the player is actually a member of your squad before eternally marking your love for him. But even that offers no guarantee of safe passage.

Newcastle fan Robert Nesbitt was so in awe of goal-scoring machine Andy Cole that he had the star's face etched on to the full length of his calf after watching Andy – now commonly known as Andrew – bang in 34 goals in 40 Premier League games in the 1993/94 season.

As with most tattoos, it takes about three weeks for the bloody scab to form, then it falls off to reveal the true splendour of your new art masterpiece.

It was around about the same time that Robert's crust peeled away that Cole made a multi-million pound move to Manchester United, with the ink drying on his contract a lot more quickly, and less painfully, than it did on the back of Mr Nesbitt's leg.

So, maybe the only sure-fire football tattoo law is to go for your club's crest. Even if they change the design, the fundamentals will still be the same, and it'll just make your piece all the more cool and retro. Surely, nothing can go wrong. Can it? Say hello to a young, unnamed,

---

Bristol Rovers have only had one active member capped for the English national side. Given that Geoff Bradford marked his debut with a goal in a 5–1 win over Denmark, it is not clear why he wasn't awarded more than one appearance.

Argentinian teenager whose love for local side Boca Juniors knew no bounds.

Being the sensible chap that he was, he opted for a tattoo of the club badge, steering clear of potential player pitfalls.

Unfortunately, the tattoo artist he selected was not such an admirer of Boca. In fact, he was a fanatical follower of their most bitter rivals, River Plate, which is akin to asking Everton's Marouane Fellaini to cut your hair.

Instead of engraving the requested item, he took it upon himself to permanently mark the back of the youngster's neck with a penis.

The tattoo in question was, ironically, beautifully executed, but it didn't take away from the fact that, instead of a Boca Juniors badge, the kid is now running around with a willy on the nape of his neck.

The victim did institute legal proceedings against the offender, but I can imagine the other reason his name has been kept confidential is due to the shame of having to constantly remove his top to show every Tom, Dick (sorry) and Harry the lasting result of his sabotaged back.

All this goes to prove that two things in football are permanent: class and tattoos.

As a footnote, players themselves have often had tattoos relating to their current club before falling out of favour and moving on to pastures new, although they still act as a reminder of a welcome period of their career.

The most famous myth centres around Jamie Carragher, with the fable suggesting that he wears a long-sleeved Liverpool jersey in order to hide an Everton tattoo. Not true, I'm afraid, although he did spend his childhood in the stands at Goodison Park.

Another folk story is that referee Dermot Gallagher has a Man United tattoo on his arm, which is why he always wears long-sleeve shirts when officiating in the Premier League.

I cannot confirm or deny this scurrilous rumour, as I've never been in a room, naked, with said referee. If it ever happens, you will be the first to know.

Burnley faced Stoke City in the 1897/98 season with both sides needing a draw to guarantee First Division football the following year. The 0–0 final score, which caused a few raised eyebrows, went down in history as 'the game without a shot at goal'.

9. Martin, to Ball, to Balloon ... Goal!

There's a lot made of the '12th man' and the romantic myth that a terrace full of fanatical, decibel-busting home fans can magically suck the ball into the opposition's net.

From the Holte End at Villa Park to the John Charles stand at Elland Road, as fans we like to believe that we can truly make a difference, and I suppose we do, to a certain extent.

Even the most ice cool of players must require a deep breath before walking out at Anfield on a European night, with the home crowd greeting every opposition touch with deafening boos.

Wherever you go at the top level, the home fans, in full voice, can act as both an intimidating factor and a barrier halting communication between the visiting players and their manager, but, ultimately, it's up to the hosts on the pitch to score the goals.

Only on a few rare occasions can a 12th man genuinely claim to have directly changed an English football scoreline, but unfortunately none of them is available for interview, given that they tend to be inanimate objects or animals, both of which can't talk and/or have already sold their stories to *Hello!* magazine.

I have deliberately not grouped match-fixing in this

scenario as that's a different story altogether, brought about usually by those already inside the dressing room. Instead, I'm talking about how, in 2004, a coffee cup kept Derby County from being relegated from the Championship. Okay, I'm stretching the realms of reality, but only by a tad.

In the 2003/04 season, the Rams were struggling to stay in the division, and were facing another titanic battle against their Mid-Eastland's rivals Nottingham Forest. After an early goal by Paul Peschisolido, which ranks amongst the greatest names for a footballer ever, County went on to take a 2–0 lead in the most random of circumstances.

Forest defender Wes Morgan played a routine back pass to keeper Barry Roche, but as he swung his trusted boot at the ball, it took a deflection off a coffee cup that had blown on to the pitch. His sliced clearance fell straight to Peschisolido, who slotted home into an empty net, giving him his second and the coffee cup an invaluable assist.

As a result, the Reds pushed forward, allowing Derby to score again on the counter, before playing out a 4–2 win.

At the end of the season, they were a mere one point above the relegation trapdoor, leaving Walsall doomed

> **Bury**'s emphatic 6–0 Wembley whitewash against Derby County in 1903 remains the biggest winning margin in the FA Cup final to date. George Ross, Charles Sagar, William Wood and John Plant all scored, with Joe Leeming netting a double.

below them, and all because of an over-enthusiastic
medium skinny non-foam vanilla latte.

A quick-thinking match steward rescued the receptacle,
which now stands in pride of place alongside the two
league championship trophies in the Derby County
museum, and if you search hard enough you'll find some
fans who still wear their commemorative T-shirts, with a
picture of their unlikely, paperweight hero on the front of
them. True story.

Manchester City were undone in the FA Cup fourth
round in 2008 in a similar way, and it provoked then
manager Sven Goran Eriksson to come out with one of
the funniest post-match quotes of recent years.

He mused, 'I have never seen a goal like that in my life
before. We told the fourth official to get a message to the
referee to stop the game for one minute ... The referee
asked Joe Hart to clear them but he has got other things
to do and he was trying to clear them when Sheffield
attacked and in the end Michael Ball was playing a one-
two with a balloon.'

The game took place at Bramall Lane against Sheffield
United, but the 7,000-strong travelling support released
a sea of blue balloons with the slogan 'it's just like watching
Brazil' and a picture of Elano emblazoned on them.

Unfortunately, loads of them landed in the vicinity of
their own keeper, Joe Hart, and when Lee Martin crossed
the ball, it struck a balloon, changing the direction of an
otherwise innocuous pass, causing Michael Ball to air kick.
It fell straight into the path of Luton Shelton, who scored
to give United a 1–0 lead.

The home side would run out 2–1 winners, causing a

search for the man responsible for the balloons in the first place.

The enthusiasm of City fan Barry Hatch had effectively knocked his own side out of the Cup but, quite rightly, he wasn't having any of it: 'I don't think you can blame my balloons for our second-half display.'

Another '12th man' was in operation that day, only this one was a living, breathing criminal. During the game somebody snuck into the away dressing room and burgled the players' valuables, leaving City's stars doubly deflated, so to speak.

On the field, only one human 12th man has claimed to have directly changed a football game, but I lean towards the humble opinion that it's absolute baloney.

In the famous England–Scotland match at Euro 1996, when Gazza scored his glorious 'dentist chair' goal to give the home side a 2–0 victory, things could have been so different had Gary McAllister scored his penalty to make it 1–1.

However, little did they know that lurking high above the stadium in some form of aircraft was the spoon-bending psychic Uri Geller, placed there by the *News of the World*, armed with nothing but one of George Cohen's England caps and a handful of mystic crystals.

Caernarfon's roots began in 1876, after an athletics club was formed to encompass football and cricket, but one report suggests that a team existed in 1787. Locals would play football on a Sunday, as well as enjoying, rather dubiously, cockfighting.

Geller claims to have used psychokinetic energy to cause Gary Mac to miss, and, in doing so, ruined any chance he had of ever walking safely through the streets of Glasgow at night.

Seaman saved the penalty, with both players remarking on a rather untimely ball movement during the Scotsman's run up to take the spot kick.

Personally, I think there's about as much chance that Uri moved the football as there is that all five members of Girls Aloud are going to be waiting for me in a state of undress when I get home from work tonight, and I seriously doubt that's going to happen twice in my lifetime.

While I don't like Geller, I do like dogs, but it was a man's best friend that finished the career of Brentford goalkeeper Chic Brodie, in 1970, when he sustained a career-ending knee injury after colliding with a miniature pooch, who had run on to the pitch during a game.

Another shaggy dog story occurred on the final day of the 1986/87 season. Torquay were losing 2–1 to Crewe with just seven minutes remaining, a result that would have seen them relegated from the Football League.

Cue Bryn, a police dog who sank its teeth into the leg of United defender Jim McNichol, after mistaking his dash towards the touchline as an attack on his handler. The nasty wound needed 17 stitches, and the delay resulted in four minutes of added-on time, during which Paul Dobson scored an equaliser to keep Torquay United up, at the expense of Lincoln City. Now that adds a whole new meaning to the phrase 'taking one for the team'.

10. Furry Fights and Monkey Business

Football, it goes without saying, has its ugly side.

Take, for example, the bare flesh, broken noses, police charges, bad language and all-out brawls witnessed on a Saturday afternoon, caused by a small group of individuals who let misplaced passion get the better of them.

The shame and unforgivable violence I am about to refer to, however, was not caused by rioting firms or Burberry-clad hooligans, but by a bunch of grown men in animal costumes. Welcome to the fearsome and scary underworld of the football mascot. As with all fans, for the most part mascots provide family entertainment for the terraces, with their do-gooding duties extending beyond match day and into the local schools and hospitals, where they spend their own free time spreading smiles, laughter and joy.

Yet, the actions of a few bad eggs caused the Football League themselves to draw up a code of conduct in 2001 after a series of scraps and savagery.

Caersws won the mid-Wales league as an amateur side three years in a row, from 1959–1963, including a 20–1 victory over Aberystwyth in 1962.

Our first Mascot Behaving Badly is Cyril the Swan, Swansea City's nine feet tall, feathered firebrand. Alongside his duties as unofficial cheerleader and mirthmaker, he has been embroiled in pitch invasions, fist fights and close encounters of a police kind.

Most famously, he flapped his way on to the pitch during a game against Millwall, prompting club stewards to send him to the stands for the duration of the match, and costing him a grand of his own money after disciplinary action was taken. On the very same afternoon, he clashed with Zampa the Lion, ripping off his head and drop-kicking it into the crowd.

His actions prompted readers of *Match of the Day* magazine to crown him Best Mascot, and we all know that condoning violence only encourages it.

Cyril has gone on to stick his neck out on many occasions, including throwing a pork pie on to the pitch during a match against West Ham, and allegedly pushing over a woman dressed as a dog whilst waiting for the start of the famous Mascot Grand National, held annually at Huntingdon Racecourse.

Wolfie, the official mascot of Wolverhampton Wanderers, is not much better. His all-out brawl with West Bromwich Albion's Baggie the Bird during a heated Midlands derby in 1999 goes down as one of the most bloody football fights of the last century, but that's nothing compared to the time the big bad wolf was pitted against the three little pigs.

The Molineux faithful, well aware of Wolfie's street rep, could hardly believe their eyes when their mascot huffed, then puffed, then promptly attacked three people dressed as pigs, shortly before a tie with Bristol City. Out-numbered, he made pork meat of the piggies, despite the fact that they were actually appearing as part of an advertising drive for a local double-glazing firm, rather than cheerleaders of the opposing team!

Now, I suppose I can't really blame a swan for ruffling a few feathers or a wolf for attacking his mortal enemy, but I would expect much better from a policeman. Enter Bury's Robbie the Bobby, dressed as a larger-than-life Sir Robert Peel, celebrating his town links with the founder of the Metropolitan Police force. Robbie, however, is on the wrong side of the law more often than not, with a rap sheet that would cause the aforementioned local hero to turn in his grave.

At the last count, Robbie – local fan Jonathan Pollard – has been shown the red card three times, one incident coming during a midweek home game against Bristol City when he mooned the visiting fans, who join a list of supporters, including those of Stoke City, that have seen more of Robbie the Bobby than they would have ideally liked. Robbie is a firm believer in actions speaking louder than words, and is actively seeking out the title of toughest mascot in Britain.

Cardiff City's 2008 FA Cup final appearance was not without controversy. The FA stated that, if victorious, they would not nominate Cardiff for a European place on grounds of nationality. They reversed their decision after UEFA President Michel Platini fumed, 'If England don't do anything, we will.' Kanu solved the problem.

He has been charged with ripping the ears off Peterborough's man-sized rabbit, Peter Burrow, but is best known for claiming the scalp of Cardiff City's Bartley the Bluebird, prising his head off during a dust-up. I must state that I mean a foam noggin, not his real head.

Despite the right hooks and the bare bottoms, our sweaty animal fans are not always to blame.

Take Kingsley the Reading lion, for example, who became the first mascot ever to be officially red carded by a referee, during a match against Newcastle United in 2007. The story goes that referee Mike Riley gave him his marching orders for standing too close to the touchline, thus confusing the linesman, who almost flagged the big cat for being offside.

Kingsley pleaded his innocence, and was consequently not disciplined, his main defence being that none of the Reading players bore any resemblance whatsoever to an eight-foot lion. Good point, well made.

Given the evidence detailed, you can understand just why the Football League felt it necessary to act, but it's important to allow the nation's mascots the opportunity to reform, exemplified in the most implausible of fashion by Hartlepool's chief cheerleader H'Angus the Monkey.

The inspiration for the name comes from a story that claims locals once hanged a monkey during the Napoleonic wars after identifying the primate as a possible French spy.

In his day, he was known for pushing the boundaries of taste, with his list of misdemeanours including romping with a blow-up doll, pitch-side in Blackpool, along with pretending to make love to a Scunthorpe steward behind her back. Lucky girl.

Stuart Drummond was feared by rival mascots and revered by his fellow fans, becoming such a cult hero that, in 2002, he entered the town's mayoral election race. Now, many people have cruelly referred to Boris Johnson as a big ape, but in this case voters actually had the chance to elect a monkey, and that's exactly what they did. His campaign slogan was simple: free bananas for school kids, a pledge that swept him into office, narrowly beating the favoured Labour Party candidate by 522 votes. Amongst those in the Town Hall watching on in dismay as the result was revealed was Peter Mandelson.

Despite cries of horror from the halls of government, Drummond would retire his monkey suit and lead his local council for a full term, before being re-elected in 2006 by an increased majority of 10,205. The monkey, it seems, made good. His pledge to supply bananas to every pupil, however, was never honoured due to budget issues, but he did offer all schools free banana plants as a compromise.

Who knows, maybe one day we'll see H'Angus run for number 10, then we really could claim to have a monkey in charge of the nation.

Carlisle United fears global warming more than most. No defence at their ground, Bruton Park, has proved a match for the neighbouring River Petterino, which has burst its banks and engulfed the stadium on several occasions.

11. Ball Boys Make Rod for Goalkeeper's Back

There are many blatant disadvantages to playing away from home, but one of the least obvious presents itself with angelic eyes and an innocent, toothy grin. In most cases, ball boys are members of the youth team, drafted in on senior match days, in theory, to return the ball to the field of play in a swift, fair manner. In reality, this rarely happens.

Next time you are watching a match, take note of the contrast between the time it takes a ball boy to return the ball to a home player, as opposed to a visiting player. These actions can help or hinder the opportunity to take a quick throw in or corner, thus having a direct influence on the ability of a team to launch a swift attack – or not, as the case may be. Don Revie's Leeds, predictably, pioneered this tactic at its early stage.

In the closing minutes of a Northern Ireland international, I witnessed first-hand then manager Lawrie Sanchez screaming at his little helper to toss the ball he was holding into a massive, unused space between the seated stand and the pitch, in order to slow down any late surge by the European Champions-elect Spain. We won 3–2 so I'm not complaining!

Thankfully, in European football, this is about as much as the ball boy can affect a game, though there was one instance which prompted Palermo to ask the Italian League to order a replay following their 1–0 defeat to AS Roma after a little whippersnapper actually placed the ball for a corner, allowing the home side to catch their guests off guard and score. Nice work half-pint.

English ball boys, apart from the evident gamesmanship, are almost scandal-free, apart from one occasion, when Spurs were playing Famagusta in the 2007 UEFA Cup. Rather than show reluctance to return the ball, the little tyke hurled it straight at the Cypriot, catching him firmly on the particulars at an estimated speed of 76 miles per hour. The crowd cheered, the ball boy smiled and the player in question, Costas Loumpoutis, clutched his unmentionables.

To find countless cases of ball boys gone bad, you have to look to Brazil. And when I say bad, I mean evil.

Comercial were playing at home to Botafogo, and with time running out the ball boy behind the visitors' net did not even bother to fetch the ball for goalkeeper Marcao, who was anxious to restart the game. When he decided to do the job himself, the kid took the unorthodox step of cracking him one with an iron bar, akin to something out of WWE's Wrestlemania!

Interfering in the field of play seems to be par for the

Carmarthen Town was the launching point for one of Wales's most established players. Defender Mark Delaney went on to make more than 150 Premier League appearances for Aston Villa, as well as winning 36 national caps.

course in Brazil, but one ball boy went a step further by actually scoring a goal.

In September 2000 Santacruzense were losing 1–0 at home to Atletico Sorocaba in a cup competition held between teams in the São Paulo region. After a shot whizzed narrowly wide, the ball boy calmly dribbled the ball back on to the pitch and nonchalantly tapped it into the opposition net.

The gap between the original shot and junior's audacious 12-inch screamer was almost ten seconds yet, inexplicably, referee Silvia Regina de Oliveira allowed the goal to stand, which didn't exactly bolster the argument for the employment of more female referees in South America.

While most Brazilians split their sides with laughter when the footage came to light, the afflicted team did not see the funny side, with the team's vice-president Valdir Cipriani, almost at a loss for words, simply gasping, 'We were defrauded.'

As for stopping goals, ball boys in Brazil are famous for it, with countless YouTube montages bearing witness to the unlikeliest of farces. The alarming regularity with which a ball boy has entered the field of play after a keeper has been rounded by a striker has to be seen to be believed. I'm not sure what's more embarrassing, the ball boy bringing his fellow half-pint colleagues into disrepute or the fact that a professional footballer can't score past a child.

I must wrap this up by stating that the vast majority of ball boys go no further than delaying the return of the ball to an adversary by a few split seconds and, as this happens at every ground, the unfairness is cancelled out. Still, it's good to see that in Britain we encourage gamesmanship from a very young age.

Celtic is not just the first British club to win the European Cup, but is still the only British side to win it with a squad of entirely native players. Inter Milan, beaten finalists, also started with 11 home-grown players.

12. You're not Cycling any More!

With the notable exception of Argentina, everyone loves Brazil. Come World Cup time, if your team hasn't qualified or has been knocked out early doors, loyalty and love immediately transfer to the toast of world football. I'm pretty sure, without needing to employ a focus group or market research, that the team who play in the famous yellow and blue, are the most popular 'second team' on the face of the planet.

With this, however, comes a little touch of envy. Think about it. To most of us, following our national football team means decades of hurt, tempered only by rare moments of exultation. Take England as the obvious example: 1966 and a 5–1 win against Germany offer up the main emotional barriers to a whole world of unthinkable pain. Penalty shoot-out disasters, Montezuma, Croatia ... the list goes on and on. I cling on to that evening in 1982 when Gerry Armstrong fired the ball past Luis Arconada and little Northern Ireland beat World Cup hosts Spain. I also have the warm memories of three amazing 21st-century Windsor Park nights under Lawrie Sanchez, which saw us once again conquer Spain, and threw in the scalps of England and Sweden for good measure. Still, we'd run out of trees if I listed all the times when I trudged away from that very same venue, distraught, exasperated and close to inconsolable.

For every home nation fan, following our country involves metaphorically throwing ourselves in front of a speeding car, hoping that, on the odd occasion, it'll swerve in time. For the average Brazilian fan, it's more a case of opening a box of chocolates and only having to avoid the odd coffee cream.

Therefore, I thought I'd cheer myself up by finding out just one story about a Brazil fan who has reason to curse his luck. It wasn't easy. Even when they lose, they console themselves not on the shoulder of a hairy, balding ex-skinhead, but on the bosom of a Brazilian beauty. In fact, the more I think about it, the more I hate Brazil.

I finally uncovered the fable of Pedro Gatica, a 52-year-old fan who cycled from his home in (randomly) Argentina, to see his beloved Brazil play in the 1986 World Cup, which took place in the sweltering heat of Mexico.

Despite the obvious distance, concerns over his age, the dangers of cycling alone at night, the rough terrain, accommodation issues and financial problems, you can't really blame old peasant Pedro for risking life and limb to make it to Mexico.

Consider the rewards once he finally made it to

Charlton Athletic was so incensed at having to ground-share with Crystal Palace in the mid-to-late 1980s that fans formed their very own political organisation. The Valley Party ran in 1990 local elections, garnering 11 per cent of the vote, despite only having one policy.

Guadalajara: Zico, Edinho, Junior, Carlos, Careca, Julio Cesar, Josimar, Socrates, Branco ... All true marvels of the game. He would stand on that terrace, bicycle safely locked up outside, blistered, bloodied and bruised from his ordeal, but joyous and reinvigorated by the feast of football offered to him as a result of his sacrifice. Only, he never made it to a single match.

Now, at this stage you are probably assuming that Pedro Gatica met with a gory roadside fate on route to Mexico. No, he did make it to the finals, only to realise that his funds had diminished so greatly along the way that he barely had enough money for a match ticket.

Undaunted, he parked his bike against a wall and began the arduous task of haggling with a tout, in an effort to gain entry to see his heroes face Spain in their opening group game.

Unfortunately, his negotiation strategy failed, and he was forced to realise that he'd cycled all the way from Argentina to Mexico for little or no reason at all. However, it was as Pedro turned away from his protracted ticket wrangle that insult would be added to injury. Whilst he was trying to secure a pass to see his heroes, thieves had stolen his bike. The 52-year-old was now left without a ticket, without money and without a mode of transport.

What happened next is not documented. I would assume he eventually made it home and, at least on telly, watched Brazil reach the quarter-finals before losing on penalties to France, in what remains one of the greatest football matches I've ever seen. I wasn't supporting Brazil that day, given that they'd thumped Northern Ireland 3–0 in the group stage.

So, next time you're sitting on the comfortable seat of a delayed train or in the relative luxury of a match-day traffic jam, returning from an away defeat to a team you absolutely despise, think of Pedro and his incredible, pointless journey. Think of Mr Gatica, and allow yourself a small, spiteful chuckle.

Chelsea's business-class existence is nothing new. In 1957, they became the first English club side to travel to a domestic match by plane, taking to the skies and heading to the faraway destination of St James' Park, Newcastle.

3

We Could Be Heroes . . .

13. It's the Late, Late Show, and Here's Your Host

There are few less welcomed accolades in football than that of 'Super Sub'.

You may enjoy unforgettable moments of last-gasp glory, but inevitably you spend more time getting splinters in your backside than actually playing the game you love. In fact, the two words shouldn't really go together. 'Super' ... as in smashing, great, fabulous, wonderful, splendid, and 'Sub' ... as in not good enough to be in the starting line-up. If you're super, then the guys getting a game ahead of you must be bordering on immortal.

It is one of the most reluctantly accepted compliments in football, yet within its history there are some truly interesting titbits.

The phrase itself was probably cemented in the soccer dictionary thanks to Liverpool's David Fairclough, who made his second appearance for the club from the bench in a 1975 UEFA Cup game against Real Sociedad, marking the occasion with a goal. He scored 55 times in the red shirt, 18 of which came in 61 substitute

Cheltenham Town, in 1849, played host to the first ever match to officially employ three referees, two of whom were on the field, while another watched from an elevated position.

appearances, including one notable derby winner.

His most famous contribution came on a legendary Anfield night against St Etienne, in the second leg of the 1977 European Cup quarter-final. With Liverpool 1–0 down from the first leg, the ginger genius saved the day minutes before the end with a late strike to send the Reds through 3–2 on aggregate, a result that would propel them to their first ever European Cup.

Despite his place in the club's history, he regarded the Super Sub tag as a 'handicap', feeling that no performance was good enough to shake off his role as 'the next best man' for the job.

Looking back at his career, you can see why he was so cheesed off. In February 1980 he started against Norwich and scored a hat-trick, only to be sent back to the bench three days later against Nottingham Forest. You guessed it, he came on in the second half of that game . . . and scored.

In the days of one substitute, Fairclough felt that the 12th man was considered to be someone who wasn't good enough to get in the team, whereas today having a plethora of substitutes means tactics play a bigger role in managerial squad decisions.

One man more at ease with the Super Sub moniker was Ole Gunnar Solskjaer, who may have a unique reason for proving such a successful bit-part player.

While others sat on the bench dreaming, sulking or cracking jokes, Ole used to take detailed notes on the game itself, watching the manager's every move and logging the outcome of every last one of his decisions, big or small. His desire to go into coaching after his playing days meant his knowledge of any given game was almost as good as the gaffer's himself, which explains why he is currently in charge of United's reserve team.

Sir Alex Ferguson described him as 'the best substitute in the world'. However, despite his obvious dedication, I'm not sure the statistics quite support that point of view.

The 'baby-faced assassin' netted 126 times in 366 games for Man United, with 97 coming in 216 starts. He scored 29 goals in 150 substitute appearances, which is less than a 20 per cent strike rate, and four of those came in an 8–1 thumping of Nottingham Forest.

But the greatness of a Super Sub is gauged not only by his goals to games ratio, but how important those strikes actually are, and Ole's last-minute success in the 1999 Champions League final capped a quite remarkable reversal of fortunes, after Bayern Munich led for more than 90 minutes.

However, not only do I question his status as 'the best substitute in the world', I'm not even sure he was the best substitute on the field that famous night.

Enter the 'other' man, Teddy Sheringham, who not only came off the bench to score an injury-time equaliser, but moments later flicked on the corner that allowed Solskjaer to stab in from close range. I'm sorry, but one goal and one assist beats one goal.

Chester City was an English club, but not if you were watching the team play at home. Only the club offices at the Deva Stadium were actually in Blighty; the rest was in Wales. I wish the Blue Knights all the best in resurrecting the club.

It gets better. Teddy replaced Roy Keane in the opening ten minutes of that same season's FA Cup final, putting United ahead 1–0 and then setting up Paul Scholes for the icing on the cake. The game finished 2–0 and, yet again, without Teddy Sheringham, the result would have been so different.

Even the most sceptical of readers is probably starting to see my point, but let me make sure with one more Teddy testimony.

It's October 2001 and England are staring World Cup elimination in the face. As they struggled to break the deadlock against Greece, the two-goal win they desperately needed was looking more and more remote. Until, that is, the substitute board went up. Arise, Sir Teddy. Within seconds of his introduction he put England 1–0 up, a contribution largely forgotten due to David Beckham's other-worldly last-gasp free kick.

If you get a spare few minutes, revisit that moment. Not only will you realise that Sheringham won the free kick in the first place, but also observe which player vitally draws away the defender in order to create the gap for Becks's sweet strike.

For me, Teddy Sheringham, in terms of important goals and assists, is the most super of the Super Subs.

There are others outside English football who, when it comes to one-off contributions, could take me to court for libel.

Dieter Muller, no relation to German goal machine Gerd Muller, made his international debut from the bench in the 1976 European Championships, being introduced in the 79th minute with West Germany losing

2–1 to Yugoslavia. Hardly an inspiring substitution, you would imagine, but Herr Dieter not only equalised a minute after coming on, but scored two more in extra time to complete a hat-trick and see his side through 4–2 on the night.

At Ibrox, in 2005, Hibernian introduced a young player called Ivan Sproule in the 62nd minute with the game locked at 0–0. He promptly went on to take Glasgow Rangers apart, scoring a quite breathtaking treble. Not many players have bagged three against Rangers, but a young St Johnstone player did manage it in 1963. His name was Alex Ferguson. Yeah, same one.

It's important not to discount the fact that Super Subs would not exist without the managers who make the actual changes, and the best example of this came in the Euro 2000 final, when French boss Roger Lemerre introduced three players who would all play a huge part in France being crowned champions. Sub number one, Sylvain Wiltord, slammed home a late equaliser to send the game into extra time; then up stepped sub number two, David Trezeguet, to hit the golden goal winner, collecting the cross from sub number three, Robert Pires.

Back in England, the 1989 FA Cup final deserves an honourable mention, as Stuart McCall came off the bench

---

Chesterfield, in the third tier, should have reached the 1997 FA Cup final, but saw an extra-time goal disallowed against Middlesbrough. Referee David Ellery ruled it out; despite the fact it crossed the line. The game finished 3–3, and they lost the replay.

---

to score twice for Everton. Unfortunately for him, Ian Rush did exactly the same thing and Liverpool won 3–2.

I'll leave this subject with the antithesis of all those listed above, namely the 'Suicide Sub'.

There are quite a few candidates and to find the winner we have to dig deep, arriving at November 1999 and the closing stages of a match between Darlington and Swansea. Walter Boyd's first act as substitute was to rush into the Darlington box and await the arrival of a free kick. I can imagine the manager's instructions were to get straight in there and make a difference. He certainly did that.

Before the free kick was even taken, Boyd smacked Darlington's Martin Gray full whack in the face, leaving the referee with no option but to send him straight off again. Given that the game had not restarted, his expulsion was officially timed at zero seconds, quite obviously the quickest red card of all time! Proof that, for every Teddy Sheringham, there's a Walter Boyd out there, waiting in the wings, ready to cock it all up.

14. Would You Like That Giant Killing with Fries?

Up until now, I've blamed the dirtiest word ever to infiltrate our beautiful game on the Americans.

I have actually banned the use of 's*ccer' from this book, assuming that it derives from our Stateside neighbours' need for a word to distinguish between their American football and our football, just in case they couldn't make out the difference over the top of their super-sized tub of popcorn.

Not true. It's actually an abbreviation of 'association football', first used in Britain. It's all our fault.

There go my plans to compile an entire piece slating Americans for even daring to play football. I was going to slam Diana Ross for missing that novelty penalty during the opening ceremony of the 1994 World Cup, despite being only about five feet from the goal, and mock the men for commonly being outplayed and outclassed by their female counterparts.

Instead, I found myself in the unenviable position of

Cliftonville lost the 1900 Irish Cup final to Belfast Celtic, but after launching an appeal it was discovered that their opponents' goals were smaller. A replay was ordered and, with equally sized nets, Cliftonville won.

trying to find one thing, just one, that American s*ccer players have done better than any other nation . . . ever. This task was the equivalent of trying to find a teenage Chelsea fan willing to admit that football existed before the launch of the Premier League.

After hours of reading and researching, I struck gold. The USA are responsible for the single greatest giant killing in the history of football.

Okay, I can almost hear you scream Ronnie Radford from your armchair, scorer of the greatest FA Cup goal ever, and one that helped non-league Hereford topple Newcastle in 1972.

And if I listen a little more intently, I can sense a groundswell of indignation from Wimbledon fans who are still floating on cloud nine after beating Liverpool in that infamous '88 final. Sorry gents, but no dice, and the same goes for all the other Cup upsets, a load of which involved sides managed by Harry Redknapp against Manchester United.

All of these were giant killings of the highest order, but still featured, at the very least, a squad of part-time players who knew each other's game, who had understanding and familiarity on their side.

Before you start throwing Cameroon's 1–0 defeat of World Champions Argentina in the opening game of 1990 at me, or Senegal's similar 2002 feat against France, then I must stop you there. Giant killings, yes, but let's just remember that it was one team of professionals beating another.

Defending over, it's time to go on the attack . . .

It was a fairly cool, grey day in the peaceful town of

Belo Horizonte, a small community more used to the coal pit than the football pitch. The date was 29 June 1950, and the locals were revelling in being one of the main cities for the World Cup, the only time Brazil has ever hosted the tournament, despite winning it five times.

This day, however, promised less of a football match and more of a ritual slaughtering. The best team in the world, arguably, were playing undoubtedly the worst.

The USA were not even a proper football team, their squad made up of just one *real* player, and he was Scottish!

Ed McIlvenny was the only professional in their ranks, the rest were teachers, meatpackers, hearse drivers, decorators and posties – sorry, mailmen. Not only did they reside in all four corners of the continent, but they rarely trained together, if at all. The pre-match team talk was more of an introduction than a game plan.

In their previous seven outings, they had managed the glorious total of two goals, which isn't too bad until you take into account they had conceded 45 at the other end. The only reason they were in the World Cup at all was because FIFA were begging every nation in the universe to send a team due to a lack of numbers, and even then the budget was so tight that the American players had to wash their own kit.

Coleraine was crushed in its first two Irish Cup appearances against Linfield in 1948 and 1951, losing 3–0 and 5–0, but eventually won the big one in 1965, beating Glenavon 2–1 and going on to lift the prestigious trophy five times to date.

In the case of defender Charley Columbo, he had a little something extra in his holdall, namely a pair of leather boxing gloves, which he actually wore during games. Needless to say, 'Gloves', as he was affectionately nicknamed, made Vinnie Jones look like the local parish vicar.

To coin an old phrase, if the US football team of 1950 had been a horse, they would have been shot and sold for glue.

So bad were this side that their own manager, Bill Jeffrey, appointed only weeks before the game and having no real knowledge of a single squad member, whispered slightly too loudly to the press, 'We don't have a chance.'

This was an accurate statement, because in the opposite dressing room sat an English side brimming with, still to this very day, some of the greatest names ever to grace the sport: Billy Wright, Alf Ramsey, Tom Finney, to name but a few.

In contrast, their pre-tournament preparation included a 6–1 demolition of a European Select XI, made up of the finest the rest had to offer.

In the group stage, they'd already despatched Chile at a stroll, while the USA had toiled their way to a 3–1 defeat at the hands of Spain.

Most experts indulged in heated arguments as to how many times England would score, opinion swinging between 12 and 385 goals.

With one eye already on the next stage, they chose to leave the best player in the world, Stanley Matthews, on the bench. Maybe this was the insult that sparked the fire in the belly of the Americans, who had no real reason to put themselves on the line, given that hardly a single person in their own country even knew they were competing. Win, lose or draw, they were destined to pack up their bags quietly and head home to a deathly silence.

With little motivation, they took the lead in the 40th minute, after a shot turned cross from PE teacher Walter Bahr was met by the diving head of a dishwasher from New York, Joseph Gaetjens. At least now they would have a goal to be proud of, no matter what happened in the second half.

However, the equaliser never came. Rather than defend, they continued to attack, whilst at the other end keeper Frank Borghi was having the game of his life. Time after time he pulled off fantasy saves to keep the superstars at bay, helped at times by a rather eccentric defence.

Eight minutes from time, Blackpool's Stan Mortenson was bearing down on goal, only for good old Gloves to clobber him in what many described as something more suited to the Super Bowl than the World Cup. The referee judged the tackle to be millimetres outside the box, and with Borghi pulling off a wonder save from the resulting free kick, England's spirit, along with a selection of Mortenson's limbs, had been broken.

In the States, not even those who cared about this strange sport they call s*ccer dared not to believe the

---

Coventry City's official club song, 'Sky Blue Anthem', was co-written by none other than player, manager and long-faced pundit Jimmy Hill. In 1962, as manager, he helped pen the classic line, 'Oysters or anyone, they shan't defeat us'.

result. The *New York Times* actually binned a wire report because they assumed it was a hoax, whilst back in England the scoreline was blamed on a misprint!

No giant killing in the history of football has ever shown such pre-match disparity between the two teams involved. So much so that no one, bar the 30,000 locals and the players on the field, believed the final score.

That's one thing that the Americans have done better than any other s*ccer-playing nation, but you can't take Ross away from me. Diana, you suck at penalties.

15. Roy, Lawrie and the Unbelievable Truth

Anyone who belittles the FA Cup deserves to be issued with a lifetime ban from all British stadiums.

It is the dream factory of English football; a place where window cleaners earn a place on 'Goal of the Month', where multi-million-pound signings journey to tight, intimidating cowsheds and, for a few Saturdays at least, a nation remembers what it means to support your local team.

Every year there's a giant killing, which brings with it tales of super binmen and prehistoric fans who tearfully exclaim, 'I never thought I'd live to see this day.' Hidden amongst all this glorious folklore, there's one fairy tale to beat them all.

The story of Roy Essandoh going from his living room to scoring the winning goal in the quarter-final of the 2001 FA Cup in less than ten days, brings with it such an extraordinary set of circumstances that even Russell T. Davies himself would have trouble imagining it.

Crewe Alexandra, scooped the estimable title of Most Admired Club at the 2006 Football League Awards. At the time they were managed by Dario Gradi, a reign that lasted for 24 years.

Roy Essandoh was a master of his craft. Unfortunately, that craft was gynaecology. When not practising this particular field of medicine, he spent most of his spare time making a fanny of himself on the football pitch. With all due respect, Roy was, and still is, the definition of a journeyman footballer, so how did it come to pass that Roy Nobody became Roy of the Rovers?

Lawrie Sanchez scored the winning goal for Wimbledon in the greatest FA Cup final upset of all time, and now he found himself managing a Division Two side which had exceeded their wildest dreams. Wycombe Wanderers fans where on cloud nine, with Premiership high flyers Leicester City next in their sights. Outside the club there was nothing but pride and delirium, while inside the gates of Adams Park the physical cost of the cup run was threatening to derail the side completely. And so begins the legend of Roy Essandoh.

Sanchez was in trouble. A horrendous run of bad luck and even worse timing had left him with four strikers injured – Andy Rammell, Sean Devine, Andrew Baird and Jermaine McSporran – whilst Sam Parkin had been recalled by Chelsea after a successful loan spell. With little or no money to spend, Sanchez called a crisis meeting of staff and club officials in an attempt to magic something out of thin air.

The lifeline used was 'phone a friend', as they attempted to lure an old favourite out of retirement for one last shot at back-page glory. Sanchez believed the answer lay in Ian Wright, a man with a sense of humour who would appreciate the call to arms. And he was right. One problem though: Wrighty still hadn't recovered from an ankle injury sustained during his last days at Burnley, so he was forced to decline the invitation. As too did Gianluca Vialli, who deemed it too soon after his Chelsea departure to don a pair of boots again.

Fresh out of ideas, a deflated Sanchez and his closest allies sat silent in his Wycombe office, until Press Officer Alan Hutchinson offered up one of the most bizarre solutions in football history. At first, everybody chuckled. Maybe that was his intention, you know, to lift the mood. Either way, by the time they filed out of the room, it had been agreed that the most effective way to solve their striking crisis was to advertise . . . on Teletext.

Now, in order for a player to be able to answer that call, he would have to be aware of said advert, be out of contract, have not played in any previous stage of the FA Cup and be, well, a centre-forward. That's a shame, as I have it on good authority that Gary Lineker was a big fan of Teletext.

Essandoh's agent, who I can only assume didn't have to drop prior commitments with Eric Cantona and Jurgen Klinsmann to deal with this issue, spotted the SOS whilst, possibly, checking out what time the *EastEnders* omnibus was on the telly. He didn't even have to phone Roy to tell him the news, as he only lived in the flat above. Off went Roy's CV, riddled with footballing false starts, to take its

---

Crusaders had a wage bill to die for in their early days. After forming in 1898, the Belfast club charged their own players two pence for the honour of pulling on the shirt, with a strict policy of 'no pay, no play'.

---

place amongst the thousands of other applications. Only that wasn't the case at all. There weren't hundreds of hopefuls, not even a handful. Our Roy was the only man who replied.

An interview wasn't necessary, and I can't imagine the medical amounted to much more than checking he had a pulse and a pair of football boots. In fact, the alleged initial conversation between manager and player was hilarious:

LS: What's your name, son?
RE: Roy, boss.
LS: Okay Ray, this is what I want you to do: score a goal.
RE: Yes, boss.

Wycombe Wanderers had their striker, but even with their squad at breaking point, Roy was only named as substitute, after Sanchez gave him a run out in the league against Port Vale and deemed him 'not the worst centre-forward I've ever seen'.

The sun rose on FA Cup quarter-final day, as 60th in the Football League made their way to Filbert Street, home of sixth-placed Leicester City, for a scheduled ending of a dream. Wycombe, under the mercurial Sanchez, had other ideas.

For 76 minutes, Wanderers wowed, outwitting the Foxes in every department, fighting for every second ball, running for every lost cause and at times matching tenacity with some clean, crisp passing and clever set pieces.

Four minutes into the second half Paul McCarthy caused the nation's eyes to boggle as he headed Wanderers into the lead, only for Muzzy Izzet to equalise. It was then, you feared the worst for Wycombe. They'd thrown everything at City, they had bled for the cause, and now, surely, fitness would be their downfall.

With 14 minutes to go on the clock, Sanchez made a double substitution, with makeshift striker Keith Ryan coming off for the soon-to-become Teletext Talisman.

Just minutes later Wycombe were denied a clear penalty, causing an infuriated Sanchez to run, Carl Lewis-esque, a full 40 yards down the pitch in anger and disbelief. He was banished from the touchline and forced to watch the remainder of the game on a small television monitor in the belly of Filbert Street. From there he would witness, like millions of others, an astonishing occurrence never to be repeated in this or any other lifetime.

In added time a man called Roy Essandoh rose from eight yards out to score the deciding goal in the 2001 FA Cup quarter-final.

The following morning his name replaced Keane, Owen and Viera on the back pages of every newspaper in Britain and around the world. Just a few weeks later he was let go by Wycombe Wanderers and with that his FA Cup carriage had turned into a great big pumpkin. To this very day he continues to play non-league football, currently at Bishop's Stortford in the Conference South, and to

Crystal Palace sent more players and staff than any other club to take part in the biggest battle of them all – the Second World War – with 98 serving in the forces. Jack Rollin's book *Soccer at War* claims this was the highest sacrifice, followed closely by Wolves and Liverpool.

safeguard the well-being of ladies' unmentionables wherever he lives at any particular period of time. May all the gods, fake or otherwise, bless his very soul.

In conclusion, I would like to briefly recap. Roy Essandoh scored a giant-killing, last-gasp winning goal in the FA Cup quarter-final because four strikers were injured, one was Cup-tied, the club couldn't afford to spend, Ian Wright had a bad ankle, Luca Vialli wasn't quite ready, his agent uses Teletext, nobody else applied for the job and last, but not least, because of his sweet, sweet head. And his name should be for ever written large in FA Cup history, as a permanent reminder that long after the money and the WAGS and the Russian billionaires disappear from the face of this earth, football, thanks to the FA Cup, will still have its magic. It will still have Roy Essandoh.

16. Hello ... Quinn Cabs, Can I Help You?

Just the other night I literally bumped into a world-class English footballer in a West End nightclub.

I couldn't avoid it, as he was entering through a narrow door just as I was attempting to leave. No one was hurt, but I was most impressed at his efforts to guard his drink, with the urgency of a man defending a one-goal lead in the dying seconds of a World Cup final.

That same evening he had been leading the charge for his club in what was a massive game, yet here he was, three hours after the final whistle, concerned only with the threat of serious spillage.

With this story comes an immediate image – the overpaid, leery, drunken footballer – but the truth is he was drinking cola, and he was actually heading to the same quiet room that I had frequented after work in the name of playing a laid-back game of poker, as opposed to a roped-off area full of pink champagne and high street honeys.

> *Dagenham & Redbridge* goalkeeper Tony Roberts made his 400th appearance in 2009, despite retiring in 2000 due to a serious finger injury. However, thanks to a specially designed glove with splints in it, he rose like a phoenix from the flames.

It's not surprising that we automatically think the worst of 21st-century footballers. My goodness, they have given us enough material to work on. From roasting to rioting, from dogging to drug taking, it's safe to say that this particular breed would be bottom of our list when it comes to booking a babysitter.

Therefore, I feel it's about time somebody shed light on the rarely mentioned good deeds that many footballers have carried out, all of which fly in the face of the theory that they care more about themselves than the club or the fans for whom they play.

I have chosen to leave out stories of high-profile, heavily sponsored youth academies. Undoubtedly, they are welcomed, and David Beckham, for one, has invested his own money, but they also serve to show the players who endorse them in a sympathetic light. No matter how pure their motives, it's good PR. I have also left out talk of charity patronage, for much the same reason. In fact, I haven't gone near charity work at all, instead concentrating on random acts of kindness towards the grass roots of a club itself that have not grabbed headlines. I have made only one exception, because the good egg in question has one of the worst reputations in the game.

When not threatening his team-mates with golf clubs, it seems Craig Bellamy is not that bad a spud after all. Fairly quietly, in 2008 he set up a foundation in Sierra Leone, investing £650,000 of his own money. When asked to address the project, he simply said, 'Because of what's happened over the years with the [civil] war children haven't had any opportunity, they haven't been thrown a football, [and] they've been thrown a gun. Now we can give them a chance that their fathers or grandfathers never had. That's the buzz for me.'

Now, I know this doesn't make the whinging Welshman any less annoying on the pitch, but it certainly shows his soft centre off it.

Back to the issue at hand, there is one shining example of a money man with a heart of gold. This story would be enough to turn Ken Bates himself into a gibbering, tearful mess.

On 31 March 2007 Sunderland were playing away to Cardiff in the Championship, always a good place to go for a booze up. The Black Cat army swarmed to the Welsh capital at considerable cost, and were rewarded with a 1–0 win.

Club chairman Niall Quinn had also made the journey south and, being one to watch the pennies, he chose to fly back to the north-east that evening on a budget airline, which meant sharing a packed flight with hordes of fans.

On seeing a true legend in the departure lounge, the 80 fans booked on his flight engaged themselves in a marathon singalong of his anthem, 'Niall Quinn's Disco Pants'.

If you haven't heard it before, it ranks up there with the

> **Darlington** is the only team to lose an FA Cup tie yet still progress. When Manchester United pulled out of the 1999/2000 tournament in favour of the FIFA Club World Championship, a lucky losers' draw was held to replace them. They lost again, this time 2–1 in the third round to Aston Villa.

greatest terrace songs of all time. To the tune of the classic 'Here We Go', the lyrics are:

> *Niall Quinn's disco pants are the best,*
> *They go up from his arse to his chest,*
> *They are better than Adam and the Ants,*
> *Niall Quinn's disco pants!*

Fairly inoffensive, in football terms, but EasyJet didn't see it that way, and asked them to refrain from, well, enjoying themselves.

The song continued right through check-in and boarding, which resulted in airline staff calling in the police to remove the boisterous bunch from the aircraft. The consequent mêlée caused the flight to be cancelled, leaving the Sunderland faithful stranded in Bristol.

Quinn was allegedly furious at the over-reaction and, determined not to see his diehard comrades left high and dry, he promptly booked and paid for an army of taxis to take every single fan back to Wearside. The mileage involved, per cab, was roughly 300 miles, at a reported cost of more than £8,000 in total.

We shouldn't be surprised by such a gesture, given that the same man donated the entire £1m raised from his 2002 testimonial game straight to children's hospitals and charities. Every single penny.

Next time you chance upon a group of Sunderland fans, and they are blasting out a hearty rendition of 'Niall Quinn's Disco Pants', you may notice a slight change in the words ...

> *Niall Quinn's taxi cabs are the best,*
> *So shove it up your arse EasyJet,*
> *Fat Freddy wouldn't do it for the Mags,*
> *Niall Quinn's taxi cabs!*

While on the testimonial front, a rather personal story comes from former Leeds and Republic of Ireland full-back Gary Kelly, who donated all money raised from his swansong to cancer charities, having tragically lost his sister to the disease.

Many other footballers have forgone their final payday in order to help others less fortunate.

But what about players who give up their wages altogether? These little anecdotes prove that some footballers not only have a conscience, but a genuine grasp of how much hard-earned money the fans fork out in the name of club love.

Argentina's Mauricio Taricco never really shone at Spurs, and ended up signing a short-term six-month contract at West Ham United, after leaving on a free transfer. His first game, against Millwall, was a complete and unmitigated disaster, with the full-back pulling up with a hamstring injury after less than half an hour.

Derby County has the chance of winning silverware every time they play against their East Midlands nemesis Nottingham Forest. Despite fierce rivalry, one special bond exists between both clubs, which is why the winner of every game they play against each other takes home the Brian Clough Trophy.

93

The initial doctor's report estimated that he'd be out of action for around eight weeks, prompting Taricco to do something almost unheard of in the history of football. Not only did he feel uncomfortable taking a wage when he had hardly even played, he actually asked manager Alan Pardew to terminate his contract. He couldn't justify being paid by a club that he hadn't contributed to, so he just waltzed right into the boss's office and asked to be made redundant, not only marking an end to his Premier League career, but effectively retiring him. He now plays in the Italian minor leagues.

He said, 'If this had happened to me at Tottenham it would have been different. I was there for six years, being out for eight weeks is little in that context. For West Ham I played less than half an hour and I had agreed a deal for six months until the end of the season. I didn't want to bring them another problem having joined them to play.'

The gaffer was suitably impressed, going out of his way to pay tribute to such a selfless sacrifice. He concluded, 'This is one of the most honest acts from a player I have experienced in all my years in the game.'

Italy's Damiano Tommasi did something similar. After a decade slogging his guts and heart out for AS Roma, he picked up a career-threatening knee injury in the summer of 2004, playing for the club he adored.

With one year left on his contract, during which he was scheduled to spend the entire time in the treatment room and the operating table, he requested that a new 12-month deal be renegotiated, paying him Italy's national minimum monthly wage of 1,500 Euros.

Remarkably, he would return to action towards the tail

end of 2005, marking a recovery that baffled club officials and medical experts alike.

The question remains: why, after season upon season of service, did Tommasi feel it necessary to throw his handsome, hefty wage down the Tiber? Well, Damo? 'I did it because I love Roma and football.' Amen.

Closer to home, some players have actually handed back money to their club as a parting gift, most notably Lee Cook, who left his boyhood team, QPR, in 2007, nipping over the road to Fulham at a cost of around £2.5m. Quite a nest egg for the club he grew up supporting but, not content, Cook also gave them his £250,000 signing-on fee. Hibernian's David Murphy did the same thing when he left the Edinburgh club for Birmingham in 2008.

It may come as a disappointment to some, but this evidence suggests that for every lager-swilling, cigar-chomping, car-crashing, lady-lovin' player, there is a heart of gold lurking in the shadows of every dressing room. Makes you go all fuzzy inside, doesn't it?

Doncaster Rovers put Arsenal in the shade when it comes to season highs. In 1946/47 they set the record for season victories, winning 33 times. Unfortunately, in 1997/98 they also broke the record for defeats in a campaign, losing 34 times, which saw them relegated to the Conference.

17. Is That Steve McQueen Playing up Front for Oldham?

In 1983 Oldham's David De-Val took on a challenge that even the great Harry Houdini refused point-blank to attempt.

His mission impossible was to escape from infamous highwayman Dick Turpin's cell at York Castle, a feat thought to be impossible by even the greatest in his field. In succeeding, he cemented his position as one of the finest magicians ever to walk the earth but, unfortunately, as things stand today, he's only the second greatest escapologist in Oldham.

Ten years later he would be upstaged, not by a dashing figure in a cape, straitjacket and chains, but by a man armed with nothing more than a suit and a never-say-die attitude.

There was only one week left of the 1992/93 Premier League and Joe Royle's Oldham Athletic were eight points from safety, rooted to the bottom of the table, with just three games left to play during a hectic finale to what had been a wretched season. Rumour has it that one bookmaker was taken to hospital with hyperventilation after a punter tried to place a bet on Oldham staying up. They had already been read the last rites, with closing fixtures against second-place Aston Villa, Liverpool and fellow strugglers Southampton seemingly extinguishing any hope they had of beating the drop.

While fans planned for the following season in the Championship, Joe Royle dared to dream of the greatest escape in football history. But it was out of his hands: not only would they need a maximum nine points, but they also required Crystal Palace to earn no more than a draw from their remaining two games.

Aston Villa were massive favourites to bang the final nail in the coffin, given that their phenomenal home form included wins against top-half sides like Liverpool, Everton, Man City, Arsenal, Nottingham Forest, Blackburn and QPR, making them all but invincible on home turf.

Not only did Oldham manage to keep a clean sheet, but a solitary first-half goal by Nick Henry and a lot of last-ditch defending kick-started a potential miracle.

In an added twist, this win clinched the title for Manchester United, their first in 26 years, although even the newly crowned champions themselves were also beaten away by Aston Villa that season.

It was left to Liverpool's superstars to finish off the Latics at Boundary Park, and Ian Rush did what he did

---

Dundee United nearly reached the European Cup final in 1984, winning their semi-final first leg 2–0 at home, but losing 3–0 away to AS Roma in dubious circumstances. The Italians were banned for a year for attempting to bribe the referee, but not before famously losing on penalties to Liverpool in the final.

---

best, scoring two goals with ease against a tired Oldham defence. Fortunately, nobody bothered to tell striker Ian Olney, a then record signing for the club, that it was a lost cause, and he matched Rush with a brace, leaving Darren Beckford to make it three goals and another miracle three points.

Now it was very much game on, with Palace travelling to Highbury to face Arsenal, and Oldham staying in familiar surroundings to welcome the Saints. A win for them and a defeat for the London side would keep them up.

Having come this far, Royle's kings of the comeback went out and blasted four past Southampton – Pointon, Olney, Ritchie and Halle all on the score sheet – with only Matt Le Tissier managing an answer.

Le Tiss would go on to complete a second-half hat-trick which meant, at 4–3, it was squeaky bum time for a crammed Boundary Park.

Palace were getting hammered 3–0 by Arsenal, so when the final whistle did finally blow, Oldham Athletic had done what even the most deluded of fans had thought beyond fantasy.

This was, by some distance, the best 11th-hour resurrection in history, although there have been several other heart-stopping final days to rival its level of drama.

One of the most enduring, ridiculous and hysterical images in English football is David Pleat's hop, skip and jump across a football pitch, but few people can tell you what prompted the Luton Town manager to make such a fool of himself.

It's hard to describe the run-cum-dance, suffice to say

that it looked by all accounts as if an invisible dog was trying to take a chunk out of his backside.

His disco moment was the result of a 1–0 win away to Manchester City on the very last day of the season. Raddy Antic's goal kept Luton up, and saw City relegated, highlighting perfectly just how wonderful and cruel football can be in just one afternoon.

However, Pleat's dance served only to hide the real magic trick of the 1982/83 season, masterminded by a more stationary Ron Saunders at Birmingham City. They were bottom of the table, six points from safety, with six games remaining.

Their turnaround was so remarkable that, come the last day of the season, they were already home and hosed. They breezed to safety with five wins in their run in, including their first three points away from home all season. Back at St Andrews, they disposed of Everton and Spurs, completing their miraculous ascent with such ease that very few people even remember it.

If Mr Pleat hadn't temporarily transformed into John Travolta with a double hamstring injury, I'm sure more people would recall this other astonishing turnaround.

I must also touch on Roy Hodgson's magic touch at Fulham in 2008. At one stage the Cottagers were 50–1

Dungannon Swifts rise to the top tier of the Irish League is admirable, but whilst playing in the mid-Ulster league in 1993, they attracted Robbie Fowler and David James to Stangmore Park for a flagship friendly against Liverpool's Under-21 side.

against staying up, but won three away games on the bounce to beat the drop, rounded off by a 1–0 win at Fratton Park, courtesy of a Danny Murphy free kick against Portsmouth, on the final day of the season.

Without wishing to offend Bradford, Sheffield United and Carlisle fans, there's just the one more great escape I'd like to mention in detail.

In the 1993/94 season Everton were rightly regarded as dark horses for the title, but a horrendous run saw them involved in a last-day scrap for survival that involved no fewer than four teams.

Everton hosted an in-form Wimbledon, who at the time were sixth in the table, but if Southampton, Ipswich Town or Sheffield United could pull off three points away from home, then Everton, against all expectations, were gone.

As it happened, United lost 3–2 at Chelsea, the Saints were involved in a 3–3 draw with West Ham, while Ipswich's goalless encounter with Blackburn Rovers meant that only a win could spare the Toffees.

Mike Walker's side started like a pensioners' pub team, with Anders Limpar mysteriously handling inside the area for no reason whatsoever, jumping at an innocuous corner like Superman on acid. The resulting penalty was slotted home by Dean Holdsworth, but things were about to get worse.

From a cross, two Everton players took each other out of the game by going for the same ball, allowing the Dons to muster a half-decent shot goalwards. As panic and farce spread equally throughout the ranks of blue, Gary Ablett's attempted clearance found the back of his own net.

At 2–0 down, survival looked beyond them, but sneaky

Swede Limpar made amends for his basketball effort in his own box by, well, diving at the other end.

His Olympic-standard flop earned the home side a penalty, and when Graham Stuart held his nerve to score, a little light appeared at the end of the relegation tunnel.

The second half saw woodwork struck, goal-line clearances and miraculous saves at both ends, before Horne fired a 30-yard screamer past Hans Segers to level the score, but Everton were still facing the drop heading into the final ten minutes.

Not one single goal in this game could be described as run of the mill, and Paul Stewart's winner nine minutes from time was such a soft effort that you could have been forgiven for assuming that the Wimbledon goalkeeper had suffered a bout of temporary blindness.

His gaffe left Sheffield United fans, relegated as a result, to marvel at how on earth Segers didn't thwart an attempt that nine out of ten grannies could have saved. Everton's rise from the ashes came in the most bizarre of fashions, and it was a shame to see that, just one year almost to the day that Oldham Athletic completed the greatest escape of them all, the same club fell through the Championship trapdoor, thanks to Limpar et al. To date, they have not managed a return to the top flight.

Everton's stadium is the only one in the world that can genuinely claim to be holy ground. St Luke the Evangelist Church is sandwiched between the Main Stand and Gwladys Street End. Goodison Park was also the first to feature under-soil heating and a three-tier stand.

18. To Alexandra ... with Love

Loyalty is the golden goose of modern-day football, and the players who display it are loved for evermore by the home support and venomously hated by the away fans.

You'll not be surprised by the big-name examples I'm going to throw at you: John Terry at Chelsea, Liverpool's Steven Gerrard, Manchester United's Roy Keane, Tony Adams at Arsenal, Paul Gascoigne at Spurs.

On the high-profile front, David Beckham deserves an honourable mention. No, don't laugh. He stated clearly that he'd only ever play for Manchester United in England, stayed at Real Madrid to fight for his place after he was told he was surplus to requirements, and you can't really blame him for adding AC Milan to his Los Angeles Galaxy commitments.

However, one account of loyalty has always stuck in my mind since it was slurred to me over several pints on a Saturday night. I had assumed it was a bit of a tall tale, but further research has confirmed a quite remarkable story.

It's 1999 and Crewe Alexandra are rooted to the foot of the Second Division. The dark clouds are gathering over the Alexandra Stadium. Most experts, with 12 games remaining, have already consigned the Cheshire side to the scrapheap.

The problem for any small club is holding on to talented players, and at the time Crewe were resigned to losing a young 20-year-old midfielder by the name of Seth Johnson.

Several big names were trying to snap up the flourishing England prospect who had, no disrespect intended, no real business being at a club sitting rock bottom of the second tier.

Alex, faced with the same financial difficulties of any business in their position, agreed a £3m transfer with Derby County. The deal went through, with the prize for Johnson being a direct route to top-flight football, unknown riches and the prospect of catching the eye of the new England manager, which would turn out to be Kevin Keegan, following the sacking of Glenn Hoddle in that same month.

Manager Dario Gradi told his best player that the club simply could not afford to reject the bid, and that he was free to go.

Seth Johnson, however, had other ideas. Without Crewe Alexandra, he would not have been in such a position in the first place, having joined as a trainee before turning professional for them. The idea of leaving them battered, bruised and doomed to relegation, not to mention the resulting serious financial problems, stuck in his throat.

Exeter City, during a 1914 tour of South America, became the first team to play against the mighty Brazil. A Rio and São Paulo select XI beat them 2–0, and Brazilian football historians recognise this as Brazil's first ever official match.

Instead, he requested that Derby County agree to delay the deal until the end of the season, on the proviso that he remained fit and in the same shape as when they offered the mountain of cash. One bad tackle, and Johnson risked losing everything. Still, this mattered not to him as he refused to discuss the downsides and risks with all parties involved.

His unwavering loyalty changed the entire mentality of a side in trouble. From pessimism grew optimism, as word of his sacrifice spread, and served as a wake-up call to players and fans alike.

Such was the impact of his decision that, just up the road in Liverpool, a man called Danny Murphy decided to take up the chance to return to his former club on loan. Another Crewe trainee, he had moved to Anfield in the summer of 1997 and hadn't really established himself in the first team yet, but don't underestimate the effect Seth Johnson's decision had on Murphy's return.

With both these players on a mission, Crewe Alexandra enjoyed a phenomenal turnaround, beating teams away from home who had stuffed them on their own turf just months earlier.

Murphy and Johnson both starred in a run that saw them take 26 points from their final 16 games, beating the drop by one solitary point. With seven wins and five draws, their great escape made the final 15 minutes of James Bond's *Moonraker* seem understated.

One moment that will live for ever in fans' hearts took place in the third from last game of the season against fellow strugglers Bristol City, when Johnson struck a crucial winner.

With the help of Murphy, Johnson risked it all to save the club he loved. For me, he's one of the unsung heroes of football, a reminder to the rest that big money and higher profile is not an excuse to drop tools and bugger off.

If you ever have cause to travel to Alexandra Stadium, ask a Crewe fan to point you towards the Air Products Stand, and watch their facial features screw up and recoil. Despite its official name, it's known locally as the Seth Johnson Stand, paid for by the money that Derby County would eventually hand over in the summer for Seth's services. To this day, he is held in the highest regard by all Alexandra fans.

He'd go on to play for Leeds after moving for £7m, but injury curbed his potential, and he had only one England cap to his name. Still, all the medals and caps in the world cannot match the one trophy that Seth Johnson has in his cabinet ... true loyalty.

Fulham's mascot, Billy the Badger, caused controversy when he was pictured on television trying to cheer up then Chelsea manager Avram Grant. Billy was also shown the red card for break-dancing during a game against Aston Villa in 2008.

19. Outfield Players Pay the Penalty

D own at the park or in the school playground, the role of goalkeeper is, on the whole, the least coveted.

For every youngster who fantasises about saving a penalty at Wembley, there are a thousand who dream of sticking the ball past him. At my school, this often resulted in full fist fights to determine who would stand between the sticks. That's probably why I ended up in goal more often than not.

It is commonplace, in a friendly kickabout, to use the 'fly-nets' rule, during which the keeper is interchangeable, via a simple high five or passing of the gloves, thus everyone endures a stint in goal.

That's probably why we all know the basic rules of goalkeeping, from where to stand for a corner to how to shout really loud at your defence for no particular reason. Therefore, it's reasonable to assume that all of our outfield stars, growing up, had to tolerate their time in the number 1 shirt. Some of those names would be forced to call on that experience during their professional career, with drastically different results.

Now, I don't know about you, but I think an outfield player going into nets during a big game is a rare and wonderful sight, up there with matches played in snow with orange balls and on-field punch-ups between two members of the same team.

The most fruitful example of a player turning goalkeeper took place on 20 April 1991, at Maine Road, as Manchester City hosted Derby County.

Giant Irish international Niall Quinn, now chairman at Sunderland, was having a very good day. He'd volleyed in a stunning goal from outside the area, and was terrorising a struggling Rams defence.

At 2–1 up, they were pressing hard for a third, until City goalkeeper Tony Coton was sent off for a foul inside the box on a perm-headed Dean Saunders. Big Niall calmly took the gloves from the departing Tony and promptly flung himself to his left, saving the penalty and, as a result, sealing the fate of Derby, who were effectively relegated as a consequence of Quinny's heroics.

His adeptness with his hands is easily traced to his childhood, during which he played Gaelic Football, reaching the final of the 1983 All-Ireland Minor Hurling Championship. He was even offered an attractive contract to head down under as a professional Australian Rules player. In fact, after retiring as a footballer, he played Gaelic for County Kildare side Eadestown. Our Niall was a real all-rounder.

Quinn's ability to guard the 'onion bag' stretched far

Gap Connah's Quay has only won the Welsh Cup once, but what a win it was. Sadly, few can now remember the day in 1929 when they stuffed the mighty Cardiff City 3–0 in the final.

---

beyond that one single occasion. In March 1999 he scored the opening goal away to Bradford City, at a time when Sunderland were pushing hard for promotion. Shortly after his 71st-minute strike Thomas Sorenson picked up an injury and, with no substitutions remaining, Quinn once again stepped up to the plate, keeping a clean sheet despite City's onslaught in the dying minutes.

So mighty was his reputation, the Republic of Ireland didn't even bother to pick the standard three goalkeepers in their 1990 World Cup squad, instead officially naming Quinn as their third choice. Alas, Packie Bonner never picked up an injury, and Gerry Payton didn't suffer a bizarre gardening accident, so Niall had to make do with four appearances in his standard centre-forward role.

For me, he's the best stand-in goalkeeper there's ever been, but Kenny Dalglish, if given the opportunity, could have run him close. He began his schoolboy career as a promising young goalie, before moving into defence and, eventually, to the striker role, where he stumbled his way to becoming the first player to score 100 goals in both the English and Scottish leagues. What a waste of talent.

Phil Jagielka is also such an outstanding keeper that, during his time at Sheffield United, then manager Neil Warnock would often name sides without a reserve goalie on the bench, knowing that Jags would step into the breach if needed.

There are many other one-off tales of players nearly becoming heroes, including that of the legendary Bobby Moore, who was forced in goal for West Ham United in a League Cup semi-final against Stoke, after they lost their goalkeeper Bobby Ferguson. Remember, back then there was only one substitute, so reserve goalkeepers rarely existed.

Moore parried a penalty, only for Mike Bernard to slot home the rebound in what turned into a 3–2 defeat.

Some outfield players are never shy to raise their hands when a number 1 is needed, most notably Glenn Hoddle, who was no stranger to the unlikely task. On one occasion, at Old Trafford, he was thrust into goal whilst defending the Stretford End, only to be subjected to various projectiles. He once recounted the story of a snooker ball whizzing past his ear, missing him by a matter of millimetres.

However, for the most part, a player-cum-goalkeeper is a recipe for disaster. Alvin Martin, when at West Ham, led his side to an 8–1 home win over Newcastle United, scoring past three different keepers. Regular Martin Thomas started, only to be replaced first by Chris Hedworth, then by Peter Beardsley, both of whom suffered a torrid time.

In recent years Man Utd's John O'Shea and Rio Ferdinand, Chelsea's John Terry and Oldham's Dean Windass, have all enjoyed a stint, the latter keeping a clean sheet away to Leicester City on 7 February 2009. The 39-year-old stated calmly after the match, that Fabio

---

Gillingham's future was literally plunged into darkness in 2002, when the club's electricity supplier cut them off due to a £100,000 unpaid bill. The situation was resolved in time for the arrival of QPR for a pre-season friendly.

Capello should consider calling him up for the next England squad!

Finally, during the 1997/98 season, Watford stalwart Steve Palmer had sweated blood in every single outfield position for his side, so for their final home game, as a mark of respect, he started in goal, completing the full sweep. Once the match had kicked off, he swapped shirts with first-choice goalkeeper Alec Chamberlain, who had been named as an outfielder in return, thus sparing Palmer any embarrassing moments.

20. I Can Hardly Bayer to Look . . .

In 2005 I honestly considered packing in football altogether.

Not my playing career, obviously, as that started and ended with my first ever useless miss-kick of a ball; it was my life as a supporter that was in mock jeopardy.

Not because I was disillusioned with the spiralling costs of going to a game, or bored with the predictable outcome of the Premier League year after year. Instead, I almost put my replica tops away for ever because I came to the conclusion that it was never going to get any better.

In just under four months, I bore first-hand witness to two results, one involving my club team, the other my beloved national side, that led me to the conclusion that no single event thereafter would ever give me the same feeling of utter jubilation and triumph.

On 7 September 2005 I was in the South Stand at Windsor Park, Belfast, watching Northern Ireland not

---

Glenavon, in 1951/52, became the first club outside Belfast to win the Irish League title, breaking a capital city stranglehold dating all the way back to 1890. They were also the first provincial side to do the league and cup double, in 1956/57.

only defeat the mighty England 1–0, but also outclass them in almost every department. I remember, when the final whistle blew, sobbing in the welcoming arms of a similarly blubbering fat bloke from Ballymena, much in the same fashion I would have embraced a long-lost relative.

In May of that very same year, I had stood amongst the ranks of Reds who invaded Istanbul, only to see my side concede three goals in the first half of their Champions League final against AC Milan. I remember going to grab something to eat at half time, only to find that the food had run out. I was hungry, freezing and starting to sober up, but felt it my duty (like almost every other Liverpool fan in attendance) to support my team to the bitter end.

What happened next is one of the most famous stories in the history of our game and, I can assure you, it was the most surreal experience I've ever had. When Alonso tucked his penalty rebound past Dida to level at 3–3, the world turned to slow motion, like some sort of Alan Hansen analysis of a computer-simulated fantasy match. It was only the next day, standing in Lime Street watching the open top bus go by, as John Arne Riise hugged the trophy a mere ten yards from my face, that reality sank in.

I did decide to continue as a devout supporter of club and country, but have resigned myself to never having a year quite like 2005. That may turn out to be true, but having delved into the history of great comebacks, I now have renewed belief that the best may still be yet to come.

Alongside Liverpool's stand two other remarkable European Cup nights, most famously Man United's late, late show against Bayern Munich, and Real Madrid's 1985 UEFA Cup reversal against Borussia Mönchengladbach, when the Spaniards bounced back from a 5–1 first-leg defeat, to win 4–0 at home and progress on the away goals rule. Also, I feel duty bound to mention West Germany's infamous return from the dead against England in the quarter-final of the 1970 World Cup.

However, none of the above, not even 2005, can quite compare with the greatest comeback of all time. I give you West Germany's Bayer Uerdingen against East Germany's Dynamo Dresden in the 1985/86 European Cup Winners' Cup quarter final. Sexy, isn't it?

Dresden, while in the shadow of Dynamo Berlin, were comfortably the second best side in the country with a formidable European record. They were taking on an unfashionable team whose German Cup success the previous year remains the only major honour in their history. Over two legs, the general feeling was not 'if' but 'by how many?'.

After a comfortable 2–0 home win, a whole host of international players were kitted up and ready to seal the deal at Krefeld the following week. Ulf Kirsten, Mathias Sammer and Hans-Jurgen Dorner, the latter of whom was the reigning German Player of the Year, all turned out for Dynamo that evening and, predictably, they marched to a 3–1 half-time lead. That's 5–1 on aggregate.

Glentoran once turned down a local boy after a trial because he was deemed 'too small and light'. He would eventually play for the Glens, albeit as part of their centenary celebrations against Manchester United. His name was George Best.

Mission impossible is an understatement. While you can never quite rule out Liverpool, Man United or Real Madrid until the final whistle, there was not a bookie's in the land that would have taken a bet on an unfashionable Bayer comeback, and not a punter in the world willing to make such a wager.

With 57 minutes on the clock, Icelandic player Larus Gudmundsson managed to win himself a soft penalty, which Wolfgang Funkel converted.

Still, no need to panic, not even when old Guddy made it three–all in the 63rd minute, as Dynamo still had a two-goal cushion and a wealth of stars to see them through. Then came a wicked deflected goal off the big gun's unfortunately named striker Ralf Minge, and all of a sudden this little side were one strike away from levelling the score!

The home team's manager threw caution to the wind, sacrificing defenders for forwards at the risk of being turned over at the other end. Instead, with 12 minutes left, the fresh right leg of substitute Dietmar Klinger levelled things at 5–5 on aggregate.

Still, this would not see them through due to the away goals rule, but by this stage Dynamo were all over the place, visibly shell-shocked by what was unfolding before their eyes. More panic in the box saw another penalty for Bayer, and when Funkel slotted the ball home, Bayer Uerdingen had turned a 5–1 deficit into a 6–5 lead in just 23 minutes, but they weren't done just yet.

As time ran out, Wolfgang Schefer made it 7–3 on the night, 7–5 on aggregate, prompting overexcited fans to invade the pitch, as stuff of fantasy turned into reality.

Various factors conspired against Dresden that night, including early injuries to Sammer and their international goalkeeper, Jakubowski. His replacement, Jens Ramme, made several mistakes over the course of 90 minutes. Still, the result was one for Mulder and Scully's X-Files rather than the sports section.

Even Bayer's coach, Karl-Heinz Feldkamp, could not find the words:

'We said to each other, "Okay, we're out, but let us bid farewell to the Cup with dignity." No one will ever be able to explain how this turnaround occurred.'

Such humiliation for the fancied side caused their star forward, Frank Lippman, who scored in both legs, to walk straight out of the team hotel after the match and defect to the West!

Bayer Uerdingen would never experience a night of glory quite like this again. An average League One side in the 1980s, they would spend the 90s yo-yoing between Bundesliga 1 and 2. These days, they currently reside outside of the top three divisions, and are in chronic financial difficulty.

The history of football is littered with three-goal turnarounds. In fact, it's not even that rare, happening almost every year somewhere in the English league.

Whether it's the Stanley Matthews FA Cup final in

Grimsby Town, in 1951, installed Bill Shankly as manager, after Liverpool turned him down. He stayed for three years, steadying the ship after recent relegation, eventually arriving at Anfield via Workington and Huddersfield Town.

1953, Man United's 5–3 reversal against Spurs in 2001, or Portugal legend Eusebio's four-goal demolition of North Korea in the 1966 World Cup, the stories are all the same.

Bayer Uerdingen, however, didn't have the big names, the form or, it seemed, the ability to pull off such a result. There were no Thierry Henrys or Ronaldinhos, but instead Funkel, Feilzer, Feldkamp and Minge.

It may not be as attractive as Kaka and Pirlo versus Hamann and Gerrard, but it's football's greatest ever comeback, even if most of the world has never even heard about it.

4

Footballing Failures

21. Big Noses and Big Egos

In the summer of 2003 there was hardly a dry bottom in the house, as Britain sweltered in all-time record temperatures and, at last, realised that global warming has its upside, albeit short term.

Maybe Liverpool football club should use this heatwave as an excuse for temporarily taking leave of their senses, thus dropping the ball in the most spectacular fashion. The Premier League had ended in relative humiliation for the red half of Merseyside, when they finished fifth in the table, with bitter rivals Everton looking down on them from fourth position.

With Gerard Houllier in charge and Phil Thompson at his side, a cold front was descending over Anfield, with restless Kopites searching their football souls for any patience they may have had left in the tank.

Thompson was hell-bent on finding new blood but, as he searched for signings, little did he realise that the

---

Hamilton Academicals, in 1971, broke with tradition to become the first British club to sign players from behind the Iron Curtain. Chairman Jan Stepek is rumoured to have sent fridge freezers and other items from his electrical store to sweeten the deals.

answer to his prayers was right below his beautiful nose. Firstly, let me make it clear that Phil Thompson's contribution to Liverpool Football Club is beyond reproach. Cut him open, and he bleeds red. Okay, that's the worst aphorism ever, but you get the drift. He held aloft the European Cup, played in seven Championship-winning sides, and loyally assisted several managers including having a valiant spell at the helm himself as Houllier recovered from a heart attack. If every current player had half the passion and loyalty displayed consistently over the decades by Pinocchio, Liverpool's trophy cabinet would be an even more crowded affair.

However, amongst all the glory, maybe this is the scratch Thompson will never quite be able to itch. Here's the story, revealed in full by the legend himself in his fantastic autobiography.

Sporting Lisbon are playing Porto, and Thompson is in the stands to cast his eye over the cream of Portuguese youth. This is not the first time he's visited this particular file, and two players in particular have caught his eye. Both came with rapidly developing acne and bags of tricks.

Ricardo Quaresma was a gifted winger, full of flair and promise, with many scouts running out of superlatives to describe his talent. Yet it was the other kid who was being literally flung Liverpool's way, for pocket change.

His British and his Portuguese agent fell over each other to court Thompson, openly offering this spotty, greasy-haired adolescent for a modest fee – £4m to be exact – and Liverpool could have him almost immediately. As for wages, the 18-year-old wanted £1m a year, tax free. Thompson claims that herein lay the stumbling block.

Big Phil returned to Melwood (Liverpool's training headquarters), and delivered this news to Gerard Houllier, who in turn passed on the details to Liverpool's Chief Executive, Rick Parry. While Liverpool tried to work out some form of compromise, Manchester United continued their pre-season tour with a game against Sporting Lisbon, in which they were almost single-handedly destroyed.

On the plane home, the United squad took the unprecedented step of confronting their boss, urging him to sign the player responsible for inflicting the 3–1 defeat, the same teenager who was offered on a plate to Liverpool several days earlier.

And so it passed, on 12 August 2003, that Manchester United paid an inexplicable £12.24m for one Cristiano Ronaldo. When Sky Sports broke the story, Phil Thompson, sitting in one of Anfield's lounges, literally choked on his lunch.

Many questions remain unanswered in relation to this whole affair, but the only true mystery is why Liverpool didn't move heaven and earth to sign the future greatest player in the world. Was it simply more step-overs than they could handle? Did they have the foresight to predict that he may have problems controlling a Ferrari? Or maybe

---

Haverfordwest, who share their nickname 'The Bluebirds' with Cardiff City, may not be the best-known team in football, but two former squad members, Ivor Allchurch and Mel Charles, played in the Welsh side that lost 1–0 to Pele's Brazil in the 1958 World Cup quarter-final.

---

they really believed that Florent Sinama-Pongolle and Anthony Le Tallec were the future of football.

Phil Thompson, in his telling of the story, is careful not to apportion blame but, reading between the lines, I believe that he actively wanted to sign Ronaldo, which seems borne out by the endless reams of complimentary things he's said about the player ever since.

So was it a case of haggling over his wage packet? Did Ronaldo slip through Liverpool's fingers because they weren't willing to pay a little under 20 grand a week? That, it seems, is the most likely reason why Ronaldo didn't sign for Liverpool, instead heading up the M62 to their mortal enemies. He went on to play a starring role at Old Trafford, winning at least one of every possible medal available to him at club level before moving to Real Madrid in the summer of 2009 for a whopping £80 million, making him the most valuable human being in football history.

There is also the possibility that, given United's close relationship with Sporting Lisbon, the whole thing was an elaborate practical joke devised by Sir Alex Ferguson to fill up his lonely summer days with endless amusement. Either way, I'd give my left whatsit to know the full story.

All that remains is for us to speculate pointlessly as to what would have happened if Cristiano Ronaldo had signed for Liverpool. Firstly – and this goes without saying – he would have had his house burgled, but would Liverpool have won the Premier League title in those early years? In short, most likely not. United have never been a one-man team and the gap between both sides, until recently, was so big that not even the emigration of one of the world's greatest players could have quite bridged that. In fact, if any team should be cursing their luck it's Chelsea. They lost out by six and two points in 2006/07 and 2007/08 respectively. Without Ronaldo scoring, diving and dazzling in varying measures, you could argue that Chelsea could have edged it. You *could* argue that, but it's complete nonsense. It's impossible to fathom what would have happened. Ronaldo could have befriended my mate Scott Judge, a Kopite of sizeable proportion, and taken to drinking pints of vodka and orange at the Sandon pub of an afternoon.

In all seriousness, the only stonewall certainty relating to Liverpool's inability to secure his services is that it's lost them a lot of money. I spoke to a financial analyst and, after taking into account improved performance, shirt sales and image rights, he put the figure at somewhere around the 2.7 gazillion mark. On the plus side, they've saved a similar fortune in hair gel.

Heart of Midlothian were not always the bitter rivals of fellow Edinburgh side Hibernian. When Hibs were refused admission to the Scottish League, it was Hearts that broke football law by playing them in 'illegal' matches, resulting in hefty fines.

22. Shrimps, Sell-outs and Shell Suits

In an episode of the sometimes humorous 1970s US sitcom *Happy Days*, Arthur 'The Fonz' Fonzerelli attempted to jump over a shark on water skis. It was this piece of televisual nonsense that caused the show to be cancelled and, thus, the phrase 'Jumping the Shark' was born.

Football, you could argue, has almost jumped that shark on several occasions but, in one particular instance, it came closer than ever.

The leap in question was made possible on the day that Manchester City offered over 100 million quid for Brazilian midfield maestro Kaka. Now, unless Kaka was in possession of a genuine treasure map garnered from the dead clutches of Long John Silver's decaying corpse, a map guaranteed to return at least £60m of said fee to City in gold bullion and pearl necklaces, then the price placed on Kaka's head – or on any other player on the planet for that matter – was ludicrous. Thankfully, Kaka stayed at AC Milan and thus, at the very last moment, the speedboat was diverted away from the Great White, at least until Real Madrid took hold of the wheel.

This story, however, is common knowledge, so let's take a look at the other end of the spectrum; players who went for a song or, in one case, a shrimp. Let us try to determine who is the greatest bargain buy of them all.

Some of these signings involving household names are simply too stupid to believe, but first let's document some lesser-known players, such as Romanian defender Marius Cioara, who eventually quit the game because of the abuse he received from opposition fans. Given his transfer fee to Regal Hornia from UT Arad, you can hardly blame them, as they had some really meaty material to work with.

Hornia's deal breaker was, remarkably, 15kg of prime pork links – that's sausage meat to you and me. He lasted merely days, due to the verbal stuffing he received, fleeing to Spain where he took up work as a farm hand. Hopefully, they kept him away from the pig pen.

Such drama produced a wonderful quote from a Hornia official, who stated forlornly, 'Not only have we lost our sausages, we have also lost a footballer.'

To Norway now, where a young striker, Kenneth Kristensen, made the switch from Vindbjart to Floey, earning his former club a real crust(acean).

The 23-year-old's fee was his weight in shrimps. I can picture a staged weigh-in, akin to the one that occurs prior to a boxing match, with onlookers whooping and hollering as he tips the scales at 75kg.

However, both these men may not have been worth any

Hereford United was forced to change its traditional all-white strip at the tail end of the Second World War. Faced with a shortage of money and white material, the team used old blackout curtains to fashion black shorts.

more than a frankfurter or a seafood salad, so it would be wrong to say they were bargain buys. In fact, we have to look on our very own doorstep for the real logic-defying transfers.

Irish striker Tony Cascarino was rumoured to have been sold by Crokenhill to Gillingham in 1982 for a set of tracksuit tops and some corrugated iron, although he claims this to be false, instead confirming that it was vital training equipment. Indeed, a massive difference.

No such denials can be issued by three players, all of them serious contenders in the race to be crowned the greatest bargain buy ever.

I give you England and Manchester United legend Gary Pallister, a rock of a central defender who, in today's market, would go for over £20 million without question. In his early days at Billingham Town, however, he hadn't quite realised his potential and cut the figure of a lanky, awkward footballer, with an adult body desperately trying to burst out of his teenage frame.

In 1984 Middlesbrough would swoop for Pally, offering in return a set of kit, a bag of balls and, clinching the deal, a goal net. In 1989 he would journey to Old Trafford for a fee of £2.3m, which meant, at least, that Billingham Town's sell-on clause would eventually net them a whopping . . . oh, hold on, they didn't negotiate one. Numbskulls.

Upstaging GP is former Liverpool and England midfielder, not to mention part-time rapper, John Barnes.

Digger began his playing career at non-league Sudbury Court, where his mercurial trickery was usually met with a late, crunching tackle to the back of his legs. Unable to

settle, the Jamaican-born legend was anxious to move on.
Cue Graham Taylor, who could see the potential,
recognised his rare ability, and was resolved to land his
man at any cost for his improving Watford side. In 1981
Sudbury Court were offered, and accepted, a new playing
kit in return for releasing the greatest player that has ever,
or will ever, grace their playing field. Do I not like that?

Still, kits were pricey, even back then, which means you
could argue that the club saved about £500, so John
Barnes can't quite claim the trophy. Oh no.

Ian Wright is a Crystal Palace legend, with his frequent
goal-scoring fondly remembered by those who still file on
to the terraces at Selhurst Park. He scored 117 goals in
the blue and red, strikes that took the club from the
Second to the First Division. He would go on to
achieve similar status at Arsenal, becoming their second
highest goalscorer of all time, with 185 goals in just 288
games.

However, in 1985, Ian Wright himself would have
laughed at you for suggesting such a dream future. He was
working as a full-time plasterer whilst turning out for his
local side, Greenwich Borough, on his days off.

Whatever he was doing on a Sunday afternoon down
the local park was enough to catch the eye of a Palace

Hibernian was the first British club ever to compete in
European competition, reaching the European Cup semi-
finals in 1955/56 before losing 3–0 over two legs to Stade
Reims, who narrowly lost in the final to the mighty Real
Madrid.

scout and, eventually, manager Steve Coppell, who offered
him a trial.

Impressed with what he saw, he swooped for the striker,
offering up a set of weights in return. Just let me repeat
that. A set of weights. Once more. A set of weights. Now,
I was eight at the time, and it so happens that I received
a set of weights from Argos for my birthday, so I can
confirm that we're looking at about £45 if they were
anything like mine.

There are other ludicrous transfer deals. One that
deserves comment is Zat Knight, who landed at Fulham
courtesy of a boxful of tracksuits, albeit from Harrods,
thanks to a certain Mohammed Al-Fayed. However, no
signing in which money or goods exchanged hands can
quite beat Wrighty and the dumbbells.

So, is Ian Wright *the* bargain buy of all time? Well, like
everything in football, it's debatable.

Ian Rush moved from Chester City to Liverpool for
£200k, and Eric Cantona from Leeds United to Man
United for a mere £1m, which both represent quite
staggering value for money, so you could make a case for
either of these two players. You could also point to the
most prolific goalscorer in English football history, Dixie
Dean, who moved from Tranmere Rovers to Everton for
three grand, although in 1924 that was quite a wad of
cash.

But the twist in this tale comes courtesy of my mate in
the pub, who pointed out that even a bag of balls or a set
of weights is worth more than, well, nothing. And that
brings me to the free transfer, and in identifying the best
free transfer of all time, we have the greatest bargain of all

time. Spurs fans, put down the book and step slowly and calmly away, because the answer is undoubtedly Sol Campbell.

Let's leave the circumstances of his departure to Arsenal at the door. You know, the stuff about him saying he would definitely re-sign for Spurs, or the part when he was offered a higher wage than any other player at White Hart Lane and especially the bit when he said in the club programme he would never play for Arsenal.

In 2001, shielded by the Bosman ruling, Campbell made the unthinkable move to Highbury for absolutely nothing.

In his very first season, under various partnerships at the back, the Gunners won the double, and he went on to form the backbone of an Arsenal side that captured three FA Cups and two Premier league titles.

In May 2006 he became only the fifth Englishman to score in a Champions League final (for the anoraks: Teddy Sheringham, Steve McManaman, Steven Gerrard and Frank Lampard), although Barcelona eventually went on to win 2–1 at the Stade de France.

In 2008 Sol Campbell finished 15th overall in a fan vote to find Arsenal's Greatest Ever Player.

Inevitably, Arsenal would have paid Campbell an inflated wage to counterbalance his free agency, but in terms of transfer fee against achievement at a new club,

---

Huddersfield Town was the first English team to win three successive First Division titles, with only Arsenal, Liverpool and Manchester United going on to match them.

he beats them all, and it would have been all the more sweet had Arsenal received a fee from Portsmouth for the man, but it remains a fact to this day that he has never moved club, throughout his entire career, for any fee whatsoever, including his return to the Gunners.

23. How Much Is That in 'Real' Money?

'**A**nd the nominees for Worst Football Signing Ever are' ... drum roll ... how long have you got?

Since the beginning of the Premier League in 1992, ticket prices have soared, players' wages have exploded and transfer fees have gone through the roof. The phrase 'money well spent' is becoming less and less applicable by the season, while the classic chant of 'what a waste of money' has turned into more of a factual statement than a fictitious slur.

In some cases, clubs would have been better taking the transfer fee and using it for toilet paper, rather than squandering it on some of the hapless cases who have darkened their dressing rooms.

The highest price tag and the most pressure is usually placed on strikers, who are bought to do one thing and one thing only ... score. Therefore, by dividing their cost by their final tally, we can actually work out how much a club, retrospectively, paid per goal.

> *Hull City* was the first team in the entire universe to be knocked out of a cup competition on penalties. It came after a hard fought draw with Manchester United in the 1970 Watney Mann Invitation Cup semi-final.

On this front, it's hard to look beyond Andriy Shevchenko, who moved from AC Milan to Chelsea for a then record price of £30.8m.

He played 47 times amidst injuries, fitness issues and alleged fall-outs with Jose Mourinho, netting only nine times in all, which is a thumping £3,422,222 per goal. However, with the Ukrainian on £130k a week at the Blues, they would have paid in wages somewhere in the region of £15m bringing the total per goal to approximately £5,088,888. Chelsea in all likelihood were still paying some of his wages while he was on loan to AC Milan, and undoubtedly when he returned briefly before heading back to Dynamo Kiev, so my figures are approximate.

As a rule, managers should hide the chequebook when it comes to hotly tipped Ukrainian hitmen. Take Sheva's team-mate Sergei Rebrov, Tottenham Hotspur's 2000 present to their fans. Unfortunately, his goal-scoring prowess was about as evident as the Millennium bug, and he managed just one solitary successful strike every six games, which West Ham fans would have killed for . . . he managed just one in 27 for them.

At least Rafa Benitez bagged Andriy Voronin for free in 2007, but his Ukraine strain saw him farmed out to Hertha Berlin after one season and just five goals, although he's currently being given a second chance. While you can see some logic in splashing horrendous amounts of cash on a renowned goal machine, there's little excuse for Leeds United's £4.3m signing of an over-the-hill, oversized and overpriced Tomas Brolin. His contract was cancelled after two years and just five goals. He failed to impress again on his return before being sold to Dynamo Moscow, adding weight to the theory that the Premier League is where former greats come to die.

Sparing Kenyon and Abramovich's blushes, however, is one Bosko Balaban, who moved from Dynamo Zagreb to Aston Villa in the summer of 2001, but never played a full 90 minutes in the League over a period of two and a half years, instead starting in two Cup encounters and appearing as a substitute on seven occasions, chalking up a final goal tally of exactly zero. He cost £6m, was paid £3m in wages, and delivered absolutely nothing. Villa, covered in shame, released him, meaning they received not a penny back in reparation. He would go on to enjoy a successful return spell in Zagreb, and at Club Brugge, thus rubbing salt into Villa's wounds. His story makes Sergei Rebrov's stint at Tottenham Hotspur look like a screaming success.

Football's biggest misfit must surely be Juan Sebastian Veron, bought by Manchester United for £28.1m, then shipped on to Chelsea for £15m. Previously at Lazio, the Argentinian played like Maradona, but as soon as he pulled on an English club jersey, his performances more resembled Madonna. At least United got 51 games out of him, whereas Chelsea managed only 14.

Institute, despite only recently playing with the big boys, can boast Northern Ireland's Ivan Sproule as part of the family. Just months after leaving for Hibernian, he scored in his first international outing, against Estonia, with his very first touch.

While I'll deal with Winston Bogarde elsewhere in this book – for the record, I don't think he was the all-time low – one of the worst deals of recent years was not made by any of the silly money clubs, but by Everton. In 2005 they shelled out £5m for a Danish defender called Per Kroldrup, who made one start before being banished to Fiorentina.

What quite went wrong is not exactly clear. The rumours range from him carrying a serious groin injury to Everton actually signing the wrong player! Either way, he may represent the most farcical exchange of currency since Victor Lustig sold the Eiffel Tower for scrap metal.

While every club has a tale of financial woe to tell, one stands head and shoulders above the rest when it comes to consistently flushing cash down the swanny. When you look at Newcastle United's record in the transfer market, it makes you wonder whether they just put a whole lot of Panini stickers into a hat and sign the first player they pull out. Or maybe a mercurial Mackem has placed a curse on their bank account.

For my money, their riskiest moment came when they splashed out £16m for a player dogged by injury.

Since he joined in 2005, Michael Owen has struggled with fitness constantly. He broke his metatarsal, damaged his cruciate ligament, pulled his thigh, endured a double hernia operation, caught the mumps and strained his calf.

When fit, he's worth it, scoring 26 goals in 62 appearances, but over such a long period of time and for such a huge sum of money, there's no doubt the price tag hasn't matched the contribution, albeit through no fault of the player. Anyway, it's now Manchester United's treatment room that could, and probably will, see a lot of him.

Ask any Magpie who they believe is their worst bit of business, and almost all of them will say, without hesitation, Albert Luque.

In a £9.5m deal, later examined in the Stevens Inquiry into corruption in football, the Spanish striker promised so much, but in two years delivered *nada*, leaving for Ajax after just 21 league games and one solitary goal.

Now, I don't want to completely ruin the week of any Newcastle fan reading this book – after all, they are a lovely bunch of people – but the money squandered at St James' Park in recent times beggars belief.

Defender Titus Bramble cost £5m but seemed to lose his ability to play football as soon as he pulled on the black and white shirt. Marcelino cost £5m from Real Mallorca but only turned out 17 times in two and a half years. Jon Dahl Tomasson, Hugo Viana, Jean-Alain Boumsong, Faustino Asprilla and Stephane Guivarc'h cost a collective £30m and returned, in performance value, about tuppence ha'penny.

Newcastle United have a death wish when it comes to buying Premier League players, a blundering business acumen that contributed heavily to their freefall into the

Inverness Caledonian Thistle, in 2010, is the only Scottish Premier League side to have an English manager. Terry Butcher, who earned 77 caps with England, adds to his honorary Scottish credentials by also being assistant manager of the Scottish national team.

Championship. Good to see them back in the big leagues, though. If their current chairman – I won't risk a prediction – is reading this, I hear Per Kroldrup would be willing to leave Fiorentina for £11m.

24. Gone in 600 Seconds

The adult housefly leads the most cruel of lives, spending its few precious moments buzzing around people's homes, desperately trying to avoid the dreaded rolled-up newspaper. On the rare occasion they do achieve a natural lifespan, they can expect it to last somewhere between 22 and 25 days. Even then, some still find time to sit back and laugh at the predicament of the modern-day football manager.

This business doesn't have much in the way of patience, especially when it comes to the hottest seat of them all.

David Peace's account of Brian Clough's 44 days in charge of Leeds, in his book *The Damned United*, was nothing short of phenomenal, but there have been several other short-term stints, including one that lasted just minutes, that put Cloughie's in the shade.

The most untimely of them all may be Les Reed's departure from Charlton Athletic after just 41 days, given

Ipswich Town was at the heart of 1981 classic film *Escape to Victory*. John Wark, Kevin O'Calaghan, Russell Osman and Laurie Sivell played for the fictitious allied forces side, while Kevin Beattie and Paul Cooper were stand-ins for Michael Caine and Sly Stallone.

that judgement night was Christmas Eve 2006. Many happy returns.

After being promoted to the top job from the assistant's role following the sacking of Ian Dowie on 14 November, his record included a Carling Cup defeat to League Two side Wycombe Wanderers and just one League win. His plight brought the best out of the nation's hacks, who dubbed him 'Santa Clueless'. Chairman Richard Murray, however, narrowly avoided the title of 'Scrooge', as the official version of Mr Reed's departure was 'by mutual consent', which surely doesn't exist in any football reality, unless the conversation goes something like this:

CHAIRMAN: Listen, I think you are rubbish.
MANAGER: I couldn't agree more.
CHAIRMAN: Excellent. I think you should leave now.
MANAGER: Too right, can't fault you there, old bean.

Reed's brief burst makes Paul Ince's 21 games in charge at Blackburn Rovers look almost luxurious, and as for Tony Adams complaining about his lengthy three and a half months at Portsmouth, he has no idea how lucky he was!

Swansea is one city where you wouldn't want to put down a hefty deposit on a mortgage until the results start going your way. They boast two of the shortest managerial careers on record, the first of which seemed to be heading for an early bath from the moment the ink dried.

Kevin Cullis was a PE teacher with no experience in professional football, his CV consisting solely of a spell looking after the fortunes of non-league Cradley Town.

So, what inspired incoming chairman Michael Thompson to give him the job is anybody's guess.

He lasted just two games and six days. After a 1–0 home defeat to Swindon and a 4–0 thumping at Blackpool, the club stated that he had resigned his post, although Cullis claimed that was not the case. Since then, rumour has it that he was so out of his depth that he didn't even conduct the half-time team talks, instead leaving it to a senior player.

So disastrous was the appointment that outgoing chairman Doug Sharpe called off Thompson's takeover and retook the reins. Lesson learned, or at least you would have thought.

Fast-forward just one year and Micky Adams marched out on Swansea after a comparatively lengthy 13 days, during which his side lost all their three competitive games. Adams claimed that promised funds had not materialised, leaving him no alternative but to walk the plank of his own accord.

Another manager to fall foul to unlucky 13 was Johnny Cochrane, who lasted less than two weeks at Reading in 1939 due to his, shall we say, 'laid back' approach.

One player stated that before an FA Cup tie, JC walked into the dressing room chomping on a cigar and swigging a whisky, and calmly asked his players, 'Who are we playing today?'

Kilmarnock's Kris Boyd, before joining Glasgow Rangers in 2005/06, left the club in emphatic fashion. He scored with his very last kick of the ball, earning Killie a 2–1 away win at Falkirk thus delivering the perfect leaving present.

What's baffling is that Cochrane had previously led Sunderland to a League title and an FA Cup, so he had all the right credentials.

Given stories like these, it seems almost pointless informing you of the details of Sammy Lee's brief encounter as Bolton boss, or Colin Todd's 98 days at Derby, especially when there are two management stints to beat them all.

Dave Bassett went from Wimbledon to Crystal Palace and then back to Wimbledon in just under four days. The story is simple: he left Plough Lane, changed his mind, and went back. Whether or not this counts, however, is open to debate, as he never signed a contract.

What is indisputable is that the shortest managerial stretch in history is one record that will never, ever be beaten.

Leroy Rosenior had enjoyed three and a half years as manager of Torquay, between 2002 and 2006, during which he led them to promotion and, the following season, relegation.

In 2007 chairman Mike Bateson offered him the chance to return to the club as gaffer, and Leroy gratefully accepted.

As a footnote, Bateson warned his new head coach that the club was heading towards a possible takeover, and there was no guarantee that the new owners would want Leroy as manager.

No worries, thought Rosenior, confident that his early performances would be enough to tilt the tables in his favour.

That Thursday, Torquay United officially unveiled their

new manager, with the local press clamouring for pictures and one-to-one interviews with the new main man. Just ten minutes later Bateman informed Rosenior that he had agreed to sell 51 per cent of the club, and that the new bosses had made it clear that they would be bringing in new coaching staff, effectively terminating his employment on the same day he was appointed.

Rosenior said, 'It was something that I knew was going to happen but I didn't think it was going to happen after ten minutes.'

That's ten minutes, folks. Leroy Rosenior was manager of Torquay United for 600 seconds. Looking on the bright side, that technically means he was unbeaten.

By the time Alex Ferguson finally hangs up the hairdryer at Old Trafford, there is a distinct possibility that he will have outlasted over 1,000 Football League managers, given that the current total is hovering around the 960 mark.

Maybe managers should consider looking for alternative, more stable career options like, I don't know, Osama bin Laden's personal bodyguard.

Leeds United's fall from grace of late has done nothing to soften football fans' feelings towards the side. A survey in the summer of 2008 named them as the most hated club in England, beating Man United into second place and Chelsea into third.

25. Stirling Effort Lads ...
How Many Did We Lose By?

They shall grow not old, as we that are left grow old: Age shall not weary them, nor the years condemn. At the going down of the sun and in the morning, We will remember them.

The words of poet Laurence Binyon, not mine, written about our fallen war heroes, but equally applicable to those teams who have risen to the greatest heights on a football pitch; the true sporting gods.

Whether it's the 1970 Brazil side, England's World Cup winners, the famous Liverpool squad of the 1980s, Arsenal's unbeaten XI, Man United's treble-winning heroes of '99, the vintage 1960 Real Madrid team or Ajax in the early 1970s, it's the most special of lists, a timeless testament to why football truly is the beautiful game.

However, the world is made up of opposites, and for every fantasy XI there is a nightmare equivalent. While many pre-match pints have been drained debating which one team is, genuinely, the greatest, less time has been spent examining the other end of the spectrum. And for good reason.

No fan wants to revisit the moments when their beloved club caused them shame, embarrassment and heartache. Or, worse, an entire season when the performances were so abysmal that you considered donating your season ticket to charity, if it wasn't for the fact that those less fortunate than ourselves have suffered enough without having to endure even more pain.

Realistically, there are three teams in the world who have been truly, truly dreadful. Not always, but for at least a period of time.

Now, I expect that most readers will anticipate a whistle stop guide to Derby County's 2007/08 Premier League season, given that they broke almost every unwanted League record, including just one win in 38 games, a grand total of 11 points and 20 'goals for' all season.

But, compared to the worst of the worst, the Ram's 'Premiersheep' adventure just about misses the bottom three.

In reverse order, here are my candidates for the trio of worst teams ever to play football at a reasonable level. It's a journey that will end in Britain, but starts in Germany, amidst a set of extraordinary circumstances.

Hertha Berlin had been caught with their football shorts down, bang to rights, for making illegal payments to players. As punishment, the German FA demoted them from the Bundesliga, but rather than promote the next best side, they concluded that it would be politically expedient to elevate another side from the same town.

Leicester City is the unluckiest – or worst – FA Cup final team ever. They've never won the oldest association football tournament in the world, and hold the record for the most finals without a win, picking up losers medals in 1949, 1961, 1963 and 1969.

Tennis Borussia Berlin were quite handy, as were Spandauer SV, another team with real potential. Wisely, they both turned down the invitation at a time when the league was going through a transitional period.

The gap between the second and third choice Berlin-based replacements was considerable, but lowly Tasmania 1900 were damned if they were going to pass on the opportunity to join the big boys after years fighting it out in a local league.

So, with just a fortnight until kick-off of the 1965/66 season, an ill-prepared and even less equipped side returned early from their holidays and began to ready themselves for the big time.

They were to play their home matches in Berlin's Olympic Stadium, a location usually reserved for the titans of German sport.

Approximately 81,000 fans watched their opening home defeat, but by the time they lined up for their final league game against Borussia Mönchengladbach, that number had dropped ever so slightly to 827, still a record low for the Bundesliga.

The reason for dwindling enthusiasm was a record that produced just two wins in 34 games, coupled with only four draws and a staggering 28 defeats. For daring to believe, they were humbled with just eights points and 108 goals conceded, sending them back to regional football with their tail between their legs, for ever.

Some sort of consolation may come from the fact that they will always be in Bundesliga's record books, albeit for going a whole season without an away win. There was also the small matter of 15 straight home games without victory. Oh yeah, and the single worst one-off German domestic home defeat in history, a 9–0 drubbing by Meidericher SV.

Even worse than Tasmania 1900, are the team ranked dead last in world football as of February 2009. Well, that's a bit harsh, as they are tied with San Marino, Guam, Anguilla, Montserrat, Papua New Guinea and the Cook Islands, all powerhouses of the game. On saying that, they are all only tied for the wooden spoon because it's physically impossible to register a lower FIFA rating.

Still, if these seven teams held a tournament, I'd back American Samoa to finish dead last.

The results from their latest campaign, aimed at achieving qualification for the 2010 World Cup, read more like rugby scores.

It started off all right, when they narrowly fell to Tonga by a scoreline of 4–0, but after that it was all downhill. A 21–1 stuffing by the Solomon Islands was followed by a 15–0 defeat at the hands of one of the most gifted international sides in the world ... Vanuatu. Hold on ... let me check Google Maps.

Okay, I'm back. It's a small island about 400 miles north-west of Fiji, with a population of just under a quarter of a million, a little over three times more than American Samoa.

Leyton Orient was put up for sale in 1995 for the princely sum of five pounds. Lifetime fan and famous sports mogul Barry Hearn had kept the club afloat for years before finally selling up for less than the price of a packet of cigarettes.

Various demographic issues affect their ability to play to any acceptable standard, but that doesn't change the fact that they are the worst national side in world football. Hope, however, reigns supreme as this latest hat-trick of defeats marks a significant step forward. Take, for instance, their qualifier in 2001 against Australia, when Archie Thompson put 13 goals past them all by himself, and that was deemed a selfless act, given that the Aussies scored so many times that no one is quite sure of the final result. Agreement was eventually reached at 32–0, the biggest international defeat ever.

The average age of the Samoans that day was said to be 18, with the *Telegraph* reporting that the entire senior squad didn't make it in time for kick-off due to a passport mix-up, causing officials to trawl school playgrounds for youths with the relevant travel credentials and, if possible, some degree of talent. So, it was literally men against boys.

The final team on my podium of shame do not reside in a little island in the middle of the Pacific Ocean, nor are they victims of circumstance. Instead, they are simply Scottish.

East Stirlingshire, known to you and me as East Stirling, although they are not and never have been from the town of Stirling, put together five consecutive seasons of unimaginably turgid football, finishing rock bottom of the Third Division on every single occasion. They were saved from relegation only by the fact that there was nowhere lower to go.

I won't enter into too many details, as they are one of our own, but from the beginning of the 2002/03 season to the end of the 2006/07 season, East Stirling couldn't beat eggs.

Their worst run came in 2003/04 when they went a monumental 24 consecutive games without one solitary point, prompting club officials to reduce players' wages to a tenner a week.

Thankfully, they were to bounce back with a vengeance in 2007/08, beating Montrose 3–1 on the final day of the season, propelling them to a barnstorming second-from-bottom finish. Glory days.

In the 2008/09 season, East Stirling have, thankfully, turned a corner, with 14 actual wins, climaxing with heroic defeat in the play-offs. For this, we all should collectively doff our caps.

No different from any of the clubs around them, for five whole seasons they were just about as bad as it gets with no unique excuse.

The irony of it all is that one of the worst teams in football, less than 20 years previously, were managed by the great Sir Alex Ferguson, who went on his way after a falling-out with the chairman. Sack the board.

Lincoln City reached the League Two play-off every year between 2002 and 2007, but failed to win promotion on each occasion, making them holders of one of the most heart-breaking records in football.

26. Football's Own Worst Enemies

Collective responsibility is great in theory but, when you're lying face down in the dirt, wishing that the pitch would open up and swallow you whole, those words ring hollow.

Scoring an own goal leaves a player feeling more alone than Ashley Cole at the Husband of the Year awards, and it's unfortunate to note that some are better at it than others.

Not many people regard Liverpool's Jamie Carragher as a goal-scoring maestro, but he's the best in the business when it comes to busting the net. His own. While he's been on target at the right end just four times in nearly 600 appearances for the Reds, he's managed nearly double that number in the goal he's trying desperately to defend.

In his defence, anyone who witnesses Carra every week throwing himself in front of piledrivers, can see why he suffers so many tough breaks.

At the time of writing, his tally sits at a Premier League record of seven, with two coming in one home game against arch rivals Manchester United, resulting in a 3–2 defeat. He loves scoring when playing Tottenham Hotspur also, with his current total being three. Another gaffe came in the 2006 FA Cup final against West Ham United.

I can only find evidence of one Englishman who has

fared worse, and that was at the turn of the 20th century. Everton's Billy Balmer managed eight in around 300 games. Quite a strike rate!

There's never a worse time to capitulate than in a big match, with the FA Cup seeming to be a magnet for players shooting themselves in the foot. The roll of shame includes Gary Mabbutt, who scored Coventry City's winner against Tottenham in the 1987 final ... whilst wearing a Spurs shirt. Four years later and it was Des Walker's turn to seal his own team's fate, only this time is was the Lillywhites who prospered from the Nottingham Forest defender's blunder. At least when Tommy Hutchinson scored against his own team in the 1981 final, the Man City player could point to the fact that his diving header had given his side the lead against Spurs in the first place. Still, if he hadn't deflected in a last-gasp free kick, City would have won the trophy. Instead, they lost the replay 3–2.

With Liverpool winning the UEFA Cup in 2001 thanks to a doubly painful own golden goal from Alaves's defender Delfi Geli, and Chelsea beating the Reds in the 2005 Carling Cup final, after a Steven Gerrard cock-up brought about extra time, it seems that very few own goals are without significance. That's the cruellest thing about it.

> **Linfield** has benefited financially more than most from the recent popularity of the national side. They lease their Windsor Park home to Northern Ireland, which qualifies them for 15 per cent of all home gate receipts.

The most costly of all time is, sadly, all too easy to identify, given that the victim paid with his life. Andres Escobar scored against his own team, Colombia, in the group stages of World Cup 1994. On his return home, he was brutally gunned down outside a bar in the town of Medellin, in what was one of the darkest days in the history of the game.

Back on the field, the Champions League has been a Mecca for the mess up, as Roy Keane found out to his cost in 2000, as his own goal helped Real Madrid to a 3–2 victory at Old Trafford, which saw the holders crash out.

John Arne Riise managed a baffling headed goal past Pepe Reina at Anfield in the first leg of their 2008 semi-final, which eventually proved the difference after the corresponding 90 minutes at Stamford Bridge.

Jamie Pollock, on the other hand, will for ever be a QPR legend, although it's only fair to point out that he never turned out for them. Instead, he dropped a clanger against them whilst playing for Manchester City. It was the penultimate game of the 1997/98 season, and meant that what would have been a vital home win turned into a 2–2 draw at Maine Road. One game later and City were relegated to the third tier of English football for the first time ever, finishing just one point and one place behind, you guessed it, QPR.

As well as popping up at the most catastrophic of times, most experts of the own goal seem to do it in fits and spurts, rather than consistently.

Aston Villa's 1970s stalwart Chris Nicholl, also a Northern Ireland international, hit home four times in a thrilling game against Leicester City in 1976, a brace in one end and a double in the other. The game finished 2–2, with Nicholl's name being the only one on the score sheet!

In the Premier League, Richard Dunne has had enough successful attempts to merit a mention, as does Frank Sinclair, who once beat his Leicester City goalkeeper Ian Walker from 35 yards with an unexpected back pass.

But what is the greatest own goal of all time?

It came from the boot of a true legend, Johan Cruyff, while he was playing for Ajax. In a derby game against FC Amsterdam, he chest-trapped a cross, then curled the ball into the top left-hand corner of the goalmouth. Why he did this is anyone's guess, but if it had been at the right end of the park, it would have won Goal of the Season!

While Jonathan Woodgate scored an o.g. and was sent off in his Real Madrid debut, his team at least went on to win, thus ridding him of any permanent scars. Not so for Gunner Tony Adams, whose sliced effort into the Arsenal net against Manchester United prompted one newspaper to print his picture on the back page, complete with a fake pair of donkey ears. Adams tells the story brilliantly in his autobiography . . . 'I was really hurt. After that it just got worse and a month later in our next away match

Lisburn Distillery was Ireland's first ever professional football club. Formed in 1880, their first ground was constructed by filling in a nearby pond and laying a football pitch over the top.

at Middlesbrough's old Ayresome Park ground, so many carrots were thrown at me that I could have opened a fruit and veg stall.'

We will spare the blushes of any more self-destructing footballers, but I doubt the record for the most own goals in one game will ever be beaten.

It's 2001 and Madagascan side Stade Olympique l'Emyrne are playing AS Adema in a meaningless final match of a round-robin four-team play-off, due to the fact that the latter had already done enough in previous matches to secure first place.

SOE had felt hard done by in previous group encounters, in one instance being denied victory after a baffling last-minute penalty was awarded to another rival side. For them it was already over, so they kicked off this last match and proceeded to score 149 consecutive own goals, as a protest against what they saw as bias amongst officials. The opposing side, already covered in glory, just stood around inspecting their fingernails, looking rather embarrassed.

I'm not sure whether such an occurrence should go down in the history books, as it turned out to be a non-event involving only one side. If it does count, then 149–0 is easily the highest score in a single match since football was invented. In fact, it probably breaks more records than I could possibly imagine but, unfortunately, not that of the most prolific own-goal scorer of all time.

The most likely culprits would have been their goalkeeper, Dominique Rakotonandrasana, and their captain, Mamisoa Razafindrakoto, but officials and players counted only the total, rather than noting the scorers. This is a shame, because whoever did the most damage was a shoe-in for the tournament's Golden Boot.

Liverpool's love affair with music is well documented, but in the Pink Floyd song 'Fearless', you can hear a recording of Kopites singing 'You'll Never Walk Alone'. Roger Waters, who composed the song, plumped for the Reds anthem despite being a lifelong Arsenal fan.

27. Pass Me the Razor Blades

One headline most football fans will never forget waking up to is 'Robinho Signs for Man City'.

The Brazilian's journey from the Bernabeu to Eastlands caused many to check their calendar, just in case 1 April had crept up on them without their notice. Here you had one of the world's finest players leaving the most famous club in the universe to join a club who aren't, or weren't, even the biggest in Manchester.

However, there is no romance in this tale, no footballing moral to be gleaned, no story to tell your grandchildren about. Instead, it was just a grotesque example of the sugar-daddy spending power that has made the English Premier League, on the whole, a billionaires' playground, and a dumping ground for foreign debt.

Undeniably, Robinho was leaving the 'Richest Club in the World 2008', to join, well, the 'Richest Club in the World 2009', with the fortune of new owners, the Abu Dhabi-based Al-Nahyan family, estimated at somewhere around £14.5bn.

Stories of massive names genuinely signing for less fashionable clubs are almost non-existent if you factor the age of the player into the equation. Fabrizio Ravanelli floated into Dundee in 2003 in the twilight of his career and played five league games without netting once. The

White Feather, bar one good cup game against Clyde in which he bagged a hat-trick, might as well have saved the train fare from Derby.

David Beckham's move to LA Galaxy was also a money issue, so no big shakes there.

Maybe the most credible and best-known example of a great player signing for a modest club is that of Allan Simonsen, European Footballer of the Year in 1977, who joined, remarkably, second tier Charlton Athletic from Barcelona in 1982.

Still, this book is designed to uncover the lesser-known history of football and this, I can honestly say, is a doozy.

The year is 1978 and Sheffield United are enjoying another season in the Second Division, after losing top-flight status two years previously.

Manager Harry Haslam was desperate to find a saviour, and eventually targeted an unknown South American teenager. How Haslam found out about him is not entirely clear, but it is likely to have some connection to his Uruguayan assistant, Danny Bergara, who still had strong links back home.

At the time, the player in question was at Argentinos Juniors and had been overlooked for his nation's 1978 World Cup squad, but Haslam was convinced that this little midfielder could turn Sheffield United around, so

Llanelli, in 1951, made a young Jock Stein a full-time professional for the first time, offering him a weekly wage of £12. His stay was brief, to say the least, but he went on to become one of Britain's greatest ever managers.

he set off to Buenos Aires to clinch the deal.

He found himself dealing with a 'Mr Fix It' character called Antonio Rattin, a former player whose name will for ever live in English football's metaphorical hall of infamy. Rattin was the Argentinian captain sent off in England's notorious 1–0 quarter-final victory in 1966, and a ringleader of the protests that saw his players refuse to leave the pitch after the final whistle. Alf Ramsey, furious with Argentina's dirty tactics, branded Rattin and his team-mates 'animals' in a post-match interview.

Accompanying Haslam on his journey was his good friend Keith Burkinshaw, the Spurs boss, who had made the very same excursion that year too, returning triumphantly with Ossie Ardiles and Ricky Villa. On arrival, they met with Jorge Cyterszpiler, the player's personal agent, and set about agreeing the particulars of the proposed signing.

Many problems would need to be overcome, not least the physical removal of the youngster from South America to Sheffield. He was seen as the future of Argentinian football and such an early departure from the domestic scene would have been viewed as a scandal of epic proportions. Still, plans were hatched that would involve paying shady sources to smuggle the new signing out of the country.

The deal looked odds on when Argentinos Juniors vice-president Settimio Aloisio accepted, in principle, the $900,000 offer. Haslam rightly believed he had got his boy, but the asking price was unexpectedly raised by the club's board, at the eleventh hour, to $1.5m. This new transfer fee was viewed as a step too far by United's moneymen, and Haslam went back to England without his number one target. He returned, instead, with Alex Sabella from River Plate, a gifted player but one who could not single-handedly halt the team's rapid descent. By 1981 they had slipped into the old Fourth Division.

They say that one man does not a team make, but this is undoubtedly the exception to the rule, as Napoli would find out in 1987. If Haslam and Sheffield United had found that extra $600,000, they would have returned to Bramall Lane with a young man called Diego Armando Maradona, and in one transatlantic journey would have changed the history of Sheffield United for ever.

Luton Town's former director, the great Eric Morecambe, marked his appointment by growing a meagre moustache. When asked to explain why, he pointed to the sparse sprinkling of hair, claiming it was 'a football moustache – eleven a side'.

5

The X Files

28. Would the Real Luther Blissett Please Stand Up?

Of all the stories in this book, I can honestly say that none is quite as insane as this one.

Within these pages you will find drunken monkeys, homicidal referees, sacrificial lambs and penis tattoos, but you will not find anything quite as otherworldly as this.

His name is Luther Blissett, and in the early 1980s, for a fairly short period, he was one of the best strikers in the world.

His trigger-happy antics shot Watford into the top flight in 1982 and, when faced with competing against the country's best defenders, he continued to deliver. In his debut season in the old Division One, he bagged 27 league goals, beating a man called Ian Rush to the top-scorer title. As he grabbed headlines, Watford hoovered up the points, finishing second in their inaugural year with the big boys.

During that time, the hottest property in England showed that changing club colours for those of his country

Macclesfield Town's Moss Rose ground in 1996 was graced by many world-class players, but unfortunately none of them was wearing the club's blue and white: Euro '96 victors Germany used it as their training base.

held no fear whatsoever, as he helped himself to a hat-trick in his debut start for England, against Luxembourg.

Watford, realistically, could not hold on to him and, after a flurry of activity, he chose to sign for AC Milan, for a price tag of £1m. There were rumours, still told often in Italian bars, that AC Milan had, in fact, signed the wrong Number 9, meaning to snap up John Barnes. However, this is ludicrous and, arguably, racist, given the fact that they don't look anything like each other. Also, Digger was not a striker, and fulfilled little of the club's criteria at this time. On his arrival, Blissett's hot streak quickly turned to an icy shade of blue, and he spent just one nightmare season in Serie A, scoring a modest five goals in that time. Luther, however, became somewhat of a reluctant celebrity due to the number of golden opportunities he squandered.

John Foot, in his fantastic book *Calcio*, summed it up when he wrote: 'Luther became famous for his fantastic misses. When it came to not scoring, he was something of a genius.'

Just one year after leaving Watford he returned to Vicarage Road, but it's the reputation he left behind that sparks off the real, unfathomable story.

During his Italian torment, Luther suffered constant abuse from the fans, some of it typical of a terrace, and some of it much more sinister, often with racial connotations. Shortly after his departure, four well-known crime writers huddled around a typewriter and collectively wrote a spy thriller called *Q*. Rather than reveal their identities, they chose to release it under a pseudonym.

The book was a huge success, topping best-seller charts and being translated into various languages. All over the world, people own a copy of *Q . . .* by Luther Blissett. One of the aforementioned authors explained the peculiar choice of pen name. 'He was a nice Afro-Caribbean guy. His unlucky season even turned him into a target of racist jokes. The Luther Blissett Project is kind of his revenge on stupidity.' The real Luther Blissett didn't immediately feel comfortable with the fact that he had become an all-conquering novelist without having to write a single word. He said, 'It's something that I've stayed clear of; you've got no control over these kinds of things. People were saying to me you should read it, but why? It's got nothing directly to do with me. Nobody asked my permission to use my name or anything like that. But what can I do about it? They get on with it and I observe from a distance.'

A nice little tale, but only a small part of something totally mystifying. Using his name as an alias or a *nom de plume* is part of what is known as the Luther Blissett Project. Not only is it hard to explain, and almost impossible to fathom where it started, but I have to confess right off the bat that I'm not sure how much of it is even true.

What I do know is that anyone can be part of the Luther

Manchester City was the first English club to be officially recognised as 'gay-friendly'. The gay rights campaign organisation Stonewall bestowed the honour after learning of the club's active attempts to employ gay people.

Blissett Project, and all you have to do is use his name under false pretences.

The legend claims that in the 1990s a group of travelling youths got fingered for riding on a public bus in Rome without tickets. They were promptly arrested and, when asked for their names, every one of them said Luther Blissett. It is rumoured that they repeated the outrageous claim again when asked to identify themselves in court, reminiscent of the classic 'I Am Spartacus!' movie scene, although it is my understanding that Kirk Douglas was not involved.

Some say this story is invented, but what is certain is that countless groups across the world have used the moniker ever since.

Poets and critics who wish to keep their identity a secret are particularly fond of signing off with the initials LB, while it has also been adopted as a stage name by various performers. Squatters are especially prone to it, mainly those in Europe and South America, where records show that many a slippery trespasser has mystically transformed into the man they call Luther Blissett.

From this point onwards the waters become a little bit muddied, and I must stress that part of the aim of the Luther Blissett Project is to hoax the media, so it's hard to work out what to believe and what to discard.

What I have learned is that Wu Wing, a cult which allegedly conducted ritual suicide in 1999, had previously used his name and, under it, 'waged a guerrilla warfare on the cultural industry, ran unorthodox solidarity campaigns for victims of censorship and repression and –

The magic sponge didn't work on Bert . . . Broken bones, p. 19.
(Getty)

Laying down the laws . . .
Angry managers, p. 25.
(PA)

Monkey becomes
politician – no news
there . . .
Crazy mascots, p. 55.
(PA)

Andrew Cole frees
Teddy in a game of
Stick in the Mud . . .
Super subs, p. 71.
(PA)

Well done, son . . . Now pack your bags. . . FA Cup heroes, p. 83.
(PA)

Quinny at gunpoint
outside stadium . . .
Hero footballers, p. 89.
(PA)

Have you seen these men?
Luther Blissett Project, p. 161.
(PA)

Would you like a touch of mint
sauce with that, Sir Les?
Footballing rituals, p. 211.
(PA)

My boys are going to take one hell of a whipping. . . Dictators and football, p. 223.
(Getty)

Honestly, Ed, five is my limit. . . Edmundo madness, p. 243.
(Agencia O Globo)

Worst . . . Double act . . . Ever . . .
Singing footballers, p. 248.
(Mirrorpix)

Sir Stanley Matthews is on fire!
Smoking footballers, p. 253.
(Advertising Archives)

"Smooth" IS THE KEY WORD
says **STANLEY MATTHEWS**
" It is smooth ball control and timing that
score goals and win points " says the most
bewilderingly skilful soccer player the world
has ever known.

**And "SMOOTH" is
the word for Craven 'A'**

Smooth to the lips
The firm feel of cork between
your lips when you light a
Craven 'A'. Cork that cannot
stick, cannot slip, that keeps the
end of the cigarette firm and dry.

Smooth to the taste
The cork tip of a Craven 'A' keeps it
cool and easy-drawing—keeps its taste
rich and smooth to the very end.

Smooth to the throat
The fine tobacco of Craven 'A', the clean fresh-
ness of a cork tip, give you smoking
that's smoother to your throat than
any you've ever known.

**Every Craven 'A' smoker
enjoys fine cigarettes
made smoother by cork**

Smooth to the lips... *Smooth* to the taste... *Smooth* to the throat

Frank Worthington in serious training . . .
Wayward footballers, p. 261.
(Mirrorpix)

Have you ever considered a salad?
Fat Footballers, p. 266.
(PA)

Goalscorer makes two good points . . .
Women footballers, p. 284.
(PA)

Phil Neville ends up at the
other Old Trafford . . .
Hidden talents, p. 289.
(PA)

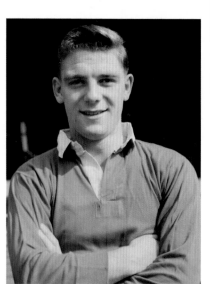

The greatest player that never was . . .
Duncan Edwards, p. 299.
(PA)

above all – played elaborate media pranks as a form of art'.

Fast-forward to 2007, and it's still happening. You may remember the reports that surfaced about hackers penetrating the offices of publishers Bloomsbury and stealing the text of the next Harry Potter book. They threatened to reveal the ending before its release, but after journalists the world over splashed the story in a huge way, a 'Luther Blissett' claimed responsibility, stating that the book was never half-inched and the whole affair was designed to prove just how easy is was to manipulate the media.

The player himself rarely comments on the phenom-enon, but seemed to see the funny side when he appeared on Euro 2004's *Fantasy Football League* show on ITV. On air he said, '*Chiunque può essere Luther Blissett, semplicemente adottando nome Luther Blissett.*'

This comes directly from a published LBP manifesto, and translates as, 'Anyone can be Luther Blissett simply by adopting the name Luther Blissett.'

So, following this instruction to the letter, it appears that anyone can be part of the LBP, by simply employing his name, although it's almost impossible to chart its correct chronological history.

One thing is for sure, I think we all owe it to the legend to continue the tradition. The next time the taxman comes round my door, I know what name I'm giving.

Words: Luther Blissett

29. Oh Keeper Where Art Thou?

Goalkeepers live in a completely different world from all other players.

In the writing of this book, two conspicuous points emerged. Firstly, goalkeepers can easily claim to be the most underrated, underpaid and undervalued members of a typical first team set-up and, secondly, they can't manage for toffee.

None of the following nuggets fits comfortably into one category, but all come together to confirm their status as a strange, and estranged, breed.

In general, they are expected to be the epitome of perfection. If they make an obvious mistake, it more often than not ends up in a goal against them, with no one behind to sweep up the mess or take the blame. Such gaffes turn them instantly into the ultimate fall guy for fans, players and the media hordes, as the old cliché of 'the keeper should have done better' returns to haunt them once again.

If you think about it, heroic goalkeepers, as the last line of defence, win matches as much as any headline-grabbing striker, so why is it that only four have ever won the Football Writers' Association Footballer of the Year award? It's just not a sexy choice, is it?

Bert Trautmann in 1956, Gordon Banks in 1972, Pat

Jennings the following year and Neville Southall in 1985 are the only victors, in a century littered with glove-wearing behemoths.

It's even slimmer pickings when it comes to PFA Player of the Year, with Jennings once again triumphant, in 1976. Peter Shilton followed in his hand-prints in 1978. That's your lot.

As for European Footballer of the Year, there have been 54 winners since 1956, with only one of them, Lev Yashin, in 1963, wearing the number 1 shirt. In order to do so, he needed to be, according to the majority of pundits, the greatest goalkeeper ever to walk the planet.

If they glance at their record books, international teams will find that their longest serving patrons patrolled the penalty box, while remaining relatively underappreciated. The net-bulging list includes the aforementioned Jennings who played 119 times for Northern Ireland, Southall made 92 outings for Wales, Andoni Zubizarreta turned out 126 times for Spain, Denmark's Peter Schmeichel leads the way with 129 and Sweden's Thomas Ravelli stars on 143.

England's Peter Shilton, despite Beckham's staying power, is England's king of the caps, while Edwin van der Sar is on a record 130 nods for Holland, a total that could still rise after his return from international retirement.

Manchester United's trophy room, despite buckling under the weight of recent successes, is missing one major trophy. Surprisingly, the UEFA Cup has never found its way to Old Trafford; a semi-final appearance in the equivalent Inter-Cities Fairs Cup in 1964/65 remains their best effort yet.

This is the same keeper who, in 2008/09, broke a host of professional club records for the number of minutes played without conceding a goal.

He was nominated for European Player of the Year, but, alas, was never taken seriously as a possible winner.

So, in short, goalkeepers are lonely, heroic and loyal during their playing days, which brings me to my other poser. Why do they rarely make decent managers?

You would think it would be the absolute opposite, given that they spend 80-something minutes of every Saturday afternoon inactively watching matches unfold before their very eyes.

However, as of August 2009, only two of all 92 English Football League clubs were under the control of an ex-goalkeeper.

Of course, there are fewer of them than outfield players, but working on a reasonable one to 11 ratio, they are massively under-represented.

Kevin Blackwell at Sheffield United and Nigel Adkins at Scunthorpe are the sole representatives, with not a single one currently in charge of a Premier League side.

Instead, many choose the role of goalkeeping coach, which has to be one of the cushiest jobs in football.

Peter Shilton's one and only foray into management was between 1992 and 1995. Things were shaping up well when he led Plymouth Argyle to the play-offs in 1994, but the following season their form slumped dramatically and Shilts was a goner.

Ray Clemence never rose higher than Barnet, while Neville Southall failed to progress beyond the dugouts of Dover Athletic and Hastings United.

Thankfully, a few have achieved glory in a nice suit, the most famous being Italy's third highest capped player of all time, Dino Zoff.

He guided Juventus to the 1990 UEFA Cup and came within seconds of becoming the first ever keeper-turned-manager to lead a national side to a European title, until France's Sylvain Wiltord's injury-time equaliser and David Trezeguet's golden goal put paid to that. What a double that would have been, given that he picked up a World Cup winner's medal in 1982 as a player.

The best goalkeeper ever to turn manager was Raymond Goethals, who transformed an unfancied Marseille side into European Champions in 1993, to add to the Cup Winners' Cup he won with Anderlecht.

Jock Wallace's reign at Glasgow Rangers during the mid to late 1970s was remarkable in that he ended bitter rival Celtic's run of nine straight League titles, but these three cases stand out from the many more tales of managerial mediocrity and failure.

On the whole, goalkeepers in their playing days stand for longevity and loyalty, albeit less appreciated, but once they hang up their gloves, it's advisable to keep them away from the manager's office, or it's likely to get ugly.

Middlesbrough has never had a foreign manager. Since turning professional in 1899, the club has gone through 28 gaffers, all of whom have been either English or Scottish.

30. Oh Brother Where Art Thou?
... Where? Macclesfield?

Even by Hollywood standards, the plot to the 1988 blockbuster *Twins*, starring Arnold Schwarzenegger and Danny DeVito, stretched people's imagination to breaking point. The notion that one brother could inherit all the desirable traits and the other the unwanted genetic debris seemed scientifically impossible.

However, as is often the case in the movie world, it appears it was actually an example of art imitating life.

Throughout football there are several cases of one brother who was front of the queue for talent, while the other was too busy swapping Panini stickers to notice his sibling drinking the gene pool dry.

We're not talking Gary and Phil Neville here, you could argue that the latter is just not quite of the same standard. Both play in the world's greatest domestic league, both have had caps in an England shirt and both are filthy rich. That's close enough. A similar case could be made for Man City's Kolo Toure and his not so little brother Yaya.

The gulf between two family members has never been drawn into such sharp focus as in 1994, when Monsieur Eric Cantona masterminded Manchester United's Double success, scoring 25 goals in one season, two of them coming in the FA Cup final against Chelsea. At the time, he was regarded by many as the best in the world. That same season, Joel, the younger Cantona, was part of the Stockport County side that made the Division Two play-off final, only to fall at the last hurdle to Burnley. When I say he was part of the side, what I mean is that he made three substitute appearances, two of which ended in rare defeats.

Poor old Joel finally managed to elevate himself to the same status as his sibling, although it wasn't on the football field. They both starred in the movie *Le Bonheur est dans le pré*, although it pains me to say that Eric, in my opinion, was by far the better actor.

However, you don't have to look to the history books for the most bizarre case of fraternal disparity. Up until his bank-busting switch to Real Madrid, the AC Milan staff list boasted not one, but two Kakas. Well, two Izecson dos Santos Leites, to be precise.

The 2007 World and European Player of the Year is the most sought-after player on the planet, borne out by Manchester City's ridiculous six-figure offer for him in the 2009 January transfer window.

His younger brother, Digão, has also been on Milan's payroll since 2007 ... not that many people have noticed.

It's fair to say that the young lad is not as naturally gifted as his big bro, and has so far been packed off on loan to Rimini in Serie B and Standard Liege. His Milan debut,

---

Millwall used to be nicknamed 'The Dockers', rather than 'The Lions', because they would kick off at 3.15 p.m. on a Saturday – later than every other side, in order to allow the local shipyard workers time to make it through the turnstiles.

in a Coppa Italia clash with Catania in December 2007, was an unmitigated disaster, with poor Digão being blamed for both of the goals in a 2–1 defeat.

Since then, he's only started once and come off the bench on another occasion, prompting press and fans alike to wonder why Milan signed him in the first place. Popular opinion is that Kaka Junior, a.k.a. Digão, may have been drafted in to stop his brother from feeling homesick. Quite a conspiracy theory, I think you'll agree, but it will all make sense if he goes on loan to Real Madrid in the near future.

Christmas dinner round at the Vieri household is another awkward one.

Christian enjoyed spells at both Inter and AC, Juventus, Lazio, Athletico Madrid and Monaco, achieving a half-century of Italy caps, nine World Cup goals and, at one stage, the luxury of being the most expensive player in the world.

His Australian-born brother Max, after failing to make the grade at Juventus, played for a long, long list of lower division Italian clubs, and chose the easier option of turning out for the Socceroos at international level.

He summed up the gulf in family flair with this rather forlorn quote: 'Of course I knew it would be hard to play for Italy. They have one of the best strikers in the world, and he happens to be my brother.'

Diego Maradona, Nicolas Anelka and Pele have all left various relatives in their wake, but closer to home there are also brotherly understudies deserving of a mention. A Welsh kid called Rhodri was part of a YTS scheme at Torquay United, before racking up a CV full of heavyweights such as Salford City, Bangor City, Bacup Borough and Mossley.

Something of a bad boy, he also enjoyed a run out in the prison yard in 2001 after being sent down for nine months on an assault charge. In 2004 the *Sunday Mirror* reported that he was roughly jettisoned from his Porsche Carrera by four masked hijackers.

His older brother, Ryan, has done slightly better for himself over the last 19 years in a Man United shirt.

To give Rod his credit, he did turn out in the red of Manchester also, although it was the Old Trafford breakaway club FC United.

Various factors could be considered as reasons for sibling inequality. There's the whole 'nature versus nurture' argument, and, as everyone knows, 'the positions of introns within the coding sequence that can be used to infer common ancestry', also come into play. (I got that from Wikipedia. I'm not even sure what it means. Sounds brilliant, though.)

Personally, as I watch Paul Terry toiling away at Leyton Orient, and John Rooney sweating blood in an effort to become a regular starter for Macclesfield, I like to remember Arnie and Danny at their best, safe in the knowledge that Hollywood is never wrong.

31. How to Score Penalties and Influence People

Next time you watch a football match through a crack in the middle of your fingers, with your stomach turning somersaults and your entire happiness hinging on one strike of a football, remember to curse the little-known figure of William McCrum.

Old Willie may not be a household name in the annals of history, but it was my fellow countryman from County Armagh, Northern Ireland, who invented the rule most likely to cause fans a coronary. And that's official.

The penalty kick is the most pressurised split-second in sport, the result of which can win trophies, break hearts, give birth to heroes and create villains to last a lifetime. In fact, after looking at the increase in hospital admissions for heart-related problems in the immediate five days after England's litany of major penalty showdowns, a study in the *British Medical Journal* stated: 'Perhaps the lottery of the penalty shoot-out should be abandoned on public health grounds.'

At least there ought to be a national holiday for the fans of Argentinos Juniors and Racing Club who, in the 1988/89 season, endured the longest-ever penalty shoot-out. After 44 spot kicks, the former eventually ran out 20–19 winners, leaving the terraces chock-a-block with chewed fingernails, gaunt faces and rapidly increasing bald patches. Who took the last penalty? The manager? The boot boy? The tea lady?

Master Willie was quite the all-round sportsman, both as an amateur player and organiser. As a member of the Irish Football Association, he was hell-bent on countering the professional foul, which was creeping into the game at that time. It was to be expected, given that there was no punishment bar an indirect free kick.

Could you imagine if the penalty kick didn't exist in today's game? The likes of Berbatov, van Nistelrooy and Torres would be permanently black and blue.

Initially, the reaction to his proposal was one of scorn and derision, with some dubbing it the 'death penalty', but in an 1891 FA Cup quarter-final, a Notts County player deliberately dived along the goal line to palm out a Stoke City shot that was destined to win them the match. This one incident is widely believed to be the reason for the sea change in opinion towards McCrum's plan.

In the beginning it was considered shameful to concede a penalty during regulation play. In one early instance, a goalkeeper for Corinthian Casuals was ordered to stand to the side of his goalmouth, therefore allowing the opposing player to roll the ball into the net uncontested, such was the stigma attached to giving away a spot kick. However, it's not the individual penalty itself, the first ever

---

MK Dons doesn't have a reserve side. As of the start of the 2008/09 season, the club decided to take the unusual step of binning its second string, concentrating only on the first team instead.

scored by Wolves' John Heath against Accrington in 1891, but the penalty shoot-out that can cause endless hours of heated debate and counter argument.

Italy won the 2006 World Cup on penalties, while the England national team prefer not to talk about them at all. In fact, even part-time football fans could probably recount the most important 12-yard strikes in domestic and international history, from Dave Beasant's save in the 1988 FA Cup final for Wimbledon, to Stuart Pearce's emphathic Wembley celebration in 1996 against Spain, exorcising, in front of millions, his ghost of Italia 90.

So, rather than retell well-worn stories of Gareth Southgate's Pizza Hut advert, I thought I would try to answer the unanswerable; are penalty shoot-outs actually a lottery?

In short, they are not. And if you don't believe me, then please don your white overcoat and grab your nearest calculator, as this book is about to go positively scientific.

In 2007 a group of boffins examined evidence from 16 teams who had all been involved in at least five shoot-outs, with at least two of them coming in major tournaments, taking in the World Cup, European Championships and Copa America. The results prove that the idea of a 'lottery' is a fallacy.

Firstly, the order of the players involved is of the utmost importance. As the pressure grows with every kick, most managers feel it important to get off to a good start, but this research shows that it's a complete nonsense. With every kick, the percentage of successful penalties decreases, from 86.6 per cent for the first attempt, down to 78.1 per cent for the last kick. Therefore, you can increase your chances of victory by simply making your fifth best kicker take the first penalty when pressure is at its lowest, and your best dead-ball player take the fifth when the pressure is at its greatest. Through some mathematical formula that I couldn't understand – in fact, it nearly caused me to abandon this article – this step turns the lottery into a battle of stats.

Pressure rules every finding, which is why squad members aged 22 or under are more than 7 per cent more likely to score than the oldies, aged 29 and above. Fresh legs also play a part, with late additions almost 7 per cent more likely to convert than those who have played through normal and extra time. Wow, this is a nerd's paradise.

My favourite titbit, however, doesn't have anything to do with age or technical ability, but is actually decided before the ball is even placed. Individualist countries are less likely to win a showdown than a collectivist nation. Put simply, the more headlines created by the individual penalty taker as an outcome of his success or failure, the more likely it is that he'll miss. David Beckham, anyone?

Also vital in maintaining an edge is to forget the goalkeeper even exists. Seriously. As part of the experiment, eggheads also asked intermediate players to take waves of penalties, half of them ignoring the

---

Morecambe manager Jim Harvey, after suffering a heart attack in 2005, was sacked on his very first day back in the job, with caretaker Sammy McIlroy being installed permanently. The men were friends and had worked together in management.

goalkeeper and the other half watching the stopper for signs of movement. Those who paid no attention to the number 1 scored more frequently than those who did, because in times of pressure a clear head with only one objective is your friend.

So, in a nutshell, pick a player who isn't headline news, has come off the bench and has only recently enjoyed puberty, and you are in with a real chance of victory! Science class is dismissed. The next time someone grumbles about losing a dreaded penalty shoot-out, politely inform him that if his team's manager had simply divided his number of players by the average age, added to that the length of time they'd been on the pitch, subtracted that figure from the nautical coordinates of the nearest fishing boat, then finally multiplied it by pi, he would easily have won that day. Or something like that.

As for alternatives to the dreaded shoot-out, many have been tried and all of them have failed.

Some suggest count backs, awarding the win to the team with the most shots, which is a direct insult to goalkeepers everywhere. Since when did a save not mean as much as a goal?

Another plan is to hold penalties before extra time, therefore encouraging the losing side to throw the kitchen sink at the winners-elect for 30 minutes. A two-year-old, I'm afraid, could work out that this is ridiculous, as the other side will close up shop and defend.

In the States (where else?), they decided to start the shoot-out from 35 yards away, with the player having five seconds' grace to hurtle towards the goal before shooting. The results were farcical.

Maybe the only viable alternative is to remove a player from each team at intervals throughout extra time, which would undoubtedly open up space and increase the chances of the game being settled in open play.

However, given that evidence suggests that skill is a prerequisite to penalty glory, maybe we should just keep things the way they are, even if it carries with it serious risk to fans' hearts and cuticles.

32. Does He Know How to Wash Dishes?

The sacred White Elephant is all but useless, as law protects it from labour. To this day, they are still kept by monarchs in countries such as Thailand and Burma, but their stagnant existence renders them almost futile, hence the birth of a common phrase.

The dictionary says that a 'White Elephant' is a valuable possession of which its owner cannot dispose and whose cost, especially upkeep, is out of proportion to its usefulness. In football, that mammal was Winston Bogarde.

His time at Stamford Bridge was all about cashing the pay-cheque, but before we look at how the Dutchman's lust for the folding green stuff rendered him an immovable object, it's important to know the back story of one of Europe's brightest young things.

After spending his early days starring for sides like SVV, Excelsior and Sparta Rotterdam, the young defender landed his dream move to an Ajax side bursting with genius.

In the 1994/95 season he lined up alongside Edwin van der Sar, Frank Rijkaard, the De Boer twins, Jari Litmanen, Patrick Kluivert, Kanu, Clarence Seedorf, Marc Overmars and Edgar Davids, and blossomed throughout a campaign that would take them not only to the league title, but also a famous 1–0 Champions League final triumph against AC Milan. A fresh-faced Bogarde was already on top of the world.

He almost repeated the feat the very next season, although the Amsterdam side lost on penalties to Juventus at the final hurdle in Europe, but he marked this year by pulling on the Orange jersey for the first time in what promised to be a long, long international career.

In 1997 he headed to AC Milan, although he was packing his bag again almost as soon as he arrived, due to various clashes with then manager Fabio Capello. In hindsight, this was an early warning sign for what was to come.

After three years and more title success with the mighty Barcelona, the talent of Holland's Winston Bogarde, now 29, was finally heading to the English Premier League.

Chelsea had swooped to secure his signature as a free agent on a four-year contract, coughing up a reported £40k a week for his services. This is where the farce begins. Firstly, Blues manager Gianluca Vialli was as surprised to see the player rock up at the Bridge as anyone else, given that he claimed to know not one single thing of the deal. It was assumed that managing director Colin Hutchinson had orchestrated the whole affair, an allegation he strongly denied. This set both men on a collision course

---

Motherwell manager Tommy McClean, in 1991, led his side to the Scottish Cup, beating Dundee United. However, his celebrations came with a slight tinge of sadness, given that the opposition manager that day was his big brother, Jim.

and, just three weeks after the arrival of Bogarde, Vialli was sacked, leaving a space for new boss Claudio Ranieri.

Even more stunned by the new signing was Chelsea's first-team coach, Graham Rix, who had actually planned an entire team performance around Bogarde's weaknesses the previous season, when they welcomed Barca in the Champions League quarter-final. It worked, with the Londoners running out 3–1 winners. When Bogarde didn't play in the return leg, Chelsea lost 5–1!

Unwanted from the beginning, Winston went on to play just 12 times in four years, 11 of which came in his first season and only four of which were as part of the starting line-up.

This offers up so many questions, the most obvious being: why, on God's earth, did he remain a Chelsea player for all that time?

Bogarde, you see, had no desire to move on. Instead, he chose to remain at the Bridge, training with the reserves and at times with the youth team; surely, a humiliating episode.

Despite being told in no uncertain terms that he was not going to get any more games for the first team, this player was not for moving, and his only motivation was money.

With no other club interested in picking up his hefty wage bill, he just sat tight and counted his riches, despite the fact that his inaction would to all intents and purposes end his career.

I mean, even Ranieri, the Tinker Man himself, wasn't interested in using him, and he loves having as many options as possible!

Still, when Bogarde's contract finally expired in the winter of 2005, he had scooped up an estimated £8.3m in payslips, for doing next to absolutely nothing. As he meandered out of the gates and disappeared into the West End of London, Chelsea fans at last got to see a glimpse of the only part of Winston Bogarde they desired: his back.

His first action, after retiring a rich man, was to invest in a Dutch concert promotions company called Global Music Entertainment, while also turning his mind to a book, titled *Deze Neger Buigt voor Niemand*. This translates as 'This Negro Bows for No One'.

In it, we find out his thoughts on his extended holiday, courtesy of Chelsea Football Club: 'Why should I throw fifteen million euro away when it is already mine? At the moment I signed it was in fact my money, my contract. Both sides agreed wholeheartedly.'

He's right, in so many words. All he did was take what he'd been offered, thus offering up the ultimate 'Exhibit A' in the case against men in suits making decisions that affect a football club on the field.

However, given his career before Chelsea, he could hardly have been short of a few bob and, in actual fact, turned down a settlement offer, which would have put, I imagine, seven figures into his bank account and allowed him to play football for another side.

Neath may be new kids on the block, but they arrived in the 2007 Welsh Premier League in true style, winning the First Division with a record 92 points.

This is why I cannot fathom out his motives, no matter how many times he attempts to explain them. 'I could go elsewhere to play for less, but you have to understand my history to understand I would never do that. I used to be poor as a kid, did not have anything to spend or something to play with. This world is about money, so when you are offered those millions you take them. Few people will ever earn so many. I am one of the few fortunates who do. I may be one of the worst buys in the history of the Premiership, but I don't care.'

I can only conclude that Winston Bogarde's passion for football must have registered somewhere around the zero mark, which answers my other big question: at what stage did one of the brightest beasts in world football turn into a White Elephant? He may have had the ability to count, but at some stage of his adulthood he obviously lost all heart, and faith, in football.

He once mused, 'If I had not succeeded as a player, I would have become a criminal.'

Some might say that wasting away on the sidelines was, indeed, a crime against football.

33. 40 New Managers a Season and We'd Win the League!

Most things in football can be measured: possession; territory; shots on target; shots off target; passes completed; tackles made; fouls committed; and on, and on, and on.

There isn't much that Andy Gray and his 'statos' at Sky Sports haven't been able to break down and deliver to you via some form of pie chart, spreadsheet, line graph or Subbutteo table.

Still, you can't rationalise every aspect of football through facts and figures, not least my favourite mystery of them all, the NME.

No, not the cutting-edge weekly music magazine that prides itself on championing new and emerging British talent, but the New Manager Effect.

How often does a struggling side sack their hapless manager after ten straight defeats only for the new guy to waltz in like some sort of Herculean magic man and promptly steamroller his first opponents? He doesn't even have to have officially taken over properly; his mere presence seems to have the desired effect.

There are no official statistics on the NME, but if anyone is ever bored and/or boring enough to go through the past one hundred years of first games in charge for professional managers worldwide, I'm sure my newly invented syndrome will measure up with ease.

Let me convey to you my very own mini-survey, centring around the English Premier League in the recent 2008/09 season.

Paul Ince at Blackburn Rovers must have cursed his luck when he realised his first game in charge was away at Everton, whose home form at Goodison Park has been the backbone to their steady success for many a season under David Moyes. Football coupons the world over had the Toffees down for a home win, but the NME effect had other ideas, with the Guv'ner enjoying a thrilling 3–2 win, heading home to Ewood Park with the sound of the fans chanting his name still ringing sweetly in his ears.

Of course, Ince would endure a torrid spell at the club, hardly having time to unpack his pencil case before being ruthlessly sacked after a horrible run of results.

Enter Sam Allardyce and a second bite of the NME cherry, this time at home to Stoke, with Rovers romping to a 3–0 win and, in the process looking like title contenders as opposed to relegation candidates.

Chelsea can go one better. While we expect more wins from them, it's still worth noting that Luiz Felipe Scolari thumped Portsmouth at Stamford Bridge 4–0 in his first game in charge, with Ray Wilkins's one match as caretaker manager producing a 3–1 FA Cup success at Watford. The trio is completed by Guus Hiddink, who faced an Aston Villa side who were threatening to shatter the Big Four monopoly. The result? Well, it was never in doubt . . . clean sheet, Anelka strike, 1–0, three points. It's as simple as that.

Although he had an easier opener, Mark Hughes began

his reign at Manchester City with a 2–0 UEFA Cup win away to EB Streymur, a Faroe Islands side who, in all honesty, my mates and I could have beaten wearing hobnail boots and straitjackets. No offence.

Not as simple was the job of Gianfranco Zola, who guided his Hammers to a 3–1 win against Newcastle during his first tricky stint in the dugout.

The list goes on and on but, unfortunately, has its exceptions.

Luckless and consequently jobless Tony Adams is one manager who could not even count on the bizarre freak of footballing nature that is the NME. He lost his first, and last, game in charge of Portsmouth to Liverpool, although when Paul Hart took over as caretaker manager he immediately registered the club's first win in two and a half months, defeating Manchester City 2–0.

Carrying on the Pompey connection, Harry Redknapp headed to White Hart Lane to take over a side bereft of any form or confidence, unthinkably languishing in a relegation spot.

Mr Houdini didn't even have to officially take charge to invoke the New Manager Effect. His appointment came so close to a game against Bolton that reserve boss Clive Allen was officially in control. Not only did they sculpt a

---

Newcastle United's record gate was due to a visiting player, rather than the home team. As a Magpie, Hughie Gallacher scored 143 goals in 174 games, provoking outrage when he was flogged to Chelsea. On his return with the Blues, 68,386 fans crammed into St James' Park to welcome him home.

2–0 win, their first league victory of the season, but they went on a run of incredible form, drawing 4–4 with Arsenal at the Emirates, before winning eight of their next ten games.

Even when managers lose their first game in charge, they usually come away with some amount of credibility. Ricky Sbragia's appointment in place of Roy Keane at Sunderland was ill-timed, given that his first Saturday was 90 minutes away to Manchester United. They lost 1–0, but the performance was markedly improved and drove them on to beat West Bromwich Albion 4–0 and a then high-flying Hull City 4–1 in their next two fixtures.

Newcastle United, however, aren't even lucky enough these days to enjoy the bizarre fruits of a new gaffer. Chris Houghton's caretaker debut, following Kevin Keegan's shock exit, saw the Magpies go down 2–1 at home to Hull, while Joe Kinnear fared only slightly better, snatching a point from Everton. Still, not much makes sense at St James' Park these days so I am damned if I am going to let them ruin my theory!

Two Championship sides from the East Midlands prove that the NME is not just confined to the big boys. No sooner was Nigel Clough installed as Derby County manager than his team were beating Manchester United at Pride Park 1–0, with Cloughie Jnr not even there long enough to meet all the players.

Nottingham Forest sacked Colin Calderwood on Boxing Day, and straight away their fortunes changed, firstly with caretaker boss John Pemberton, who masterminded an away win at Norwich, and then under

Billy Davies, who had no problem saying hello with a 2–0 away win at Charlton.

The reason why I believe the NME occurs lies in the astonishing early fortunes of England international managers. It is here that maybe we can draw more conclusions as to why new bosses seem, on the whole, to have the Midas touch.

England's last SEVEN permanent managers have all won their opening encounters, namely Fabio Capello, Steve McClaren, Sven-Goran Eriksson, Kevin Keegan, Glenn Hoddle, Terry Venables and Graham Taylor. In fact, the last full-time England boss to lose his opening game was none other than Sir Alf Ramsey in 1963.

When a new national boss is put in place, everything is immediately on the line. He has the power to change the squad, put senior players out to graze, bleed in the kids and stamp his own mark on proceedings. In fact, given the profile of this job and the smaller number of games, he's probably more inclined to do so than a club manager, at least at first. McClaren immediately dropping David Beckham is a case in point. Every team member, therefore, is not only playing for their international lives, but for the profile, sponsorship and the bags of money that go hand-in-hand with it.

At club level, a new manager often rolls out the cliché

> **Newi Cefn Druids**, originating from Druids FC, is the oldest club in Wales. In those days, they dominated, supplying six of Wales's 11 players for their first ever international fixture in 1876, when they met Scotland.

that every player starts with a clean slate, which leaves the established players in the situation of once again having to justify their place in the starting 11, and prompts the out-of-favour demotivated players to roll their socks up and give it one more try.

It is, put simply, the prospect of a second chance and the fear of being left behind that produce the New Manager Effect.

Now, if I was being cynical, I might also draw your attention to the theory that at some clubs so desperate are the players to get rid of a manager that they may deliberately underperform in order to bring about a more speedy sacking. This would certainly cause an immediate spike in form when the new man comes in as the key members of the squad naturally return to fifth gear. Surely no professional athlete would stoop so low? Would they?

34. The Scillyest League in the World

'**C**an we play you every week?! Can we play you every week? Can we play you ... can we play you ... can we play you every week?! Can we play you every week?!'

Ah yes, one of the most time-honoured and hurtful chants in football. Sung in the dying minutes by a triumphant terrace, thrilled in victory, yet hell-bent on making the misery of their deftly defeated counterparts as painful as possible.

However, there is one place on earth where this anthem is less of an insult, and more of a metaphorical question.

The Scilly Isles, with a population of just under 2,000, have enjoyed a proud tradition of league football since the end of the First World War, battling against the elements to bring competitive weekend matches to their residents. It's heroic, really.

In the 1920s teams from five separate islands fought it out over a normal season, but slowly the numbers began to diminish and, by the 1950s, there were only two teams remaining. Despite the obvious handicap, they literally did play each other every week. In fact, they still do.

The league, which is officially affiliated with the Football Association, refuses to die, which means that, to this very day, two teams play each other week in, week out. The Garrison Gunners and the Woolpack Wanderers compete

in a 17-week league programme, as well as a Charity
Shield curtain raiser and two separate cup competitions,
just like the English Premier League.

So, in any given season, you are guaranteed to reach
three cup finals and finish top or bottom of the division,
without any threat of relegation. I say give them a
Champions League spot!

You might imagine that, given the familiarity of the
competition, Scilly Isles football might get a little bit
repetitive, but not at all, because the teams never stay the
same long enough.

At the start of each season two captains are selected.
They go to the pub, have a few beers and divvy up the
eligible and willing pool of players into two evenly matched
squads for that coming season. Now there's a future
blueprint for Rangers and Celtic if ever I saw one.

While the Woolpack Wanderers are currently enjoying
a wonderful run in the Charity Shield, the competition
has never been as one-sided as to make it pointless, and
both sides utilise a 20-man squad to make sure every
fixture is honoured.

It's also made all the more exciting by the fact that they
share the same ground, perched on a hilltop and open to
the elements during a season that starts in November and
runs right through the most extreme weather the island
endures in any given year.

Such intimacy breeds a fierce rivalry, but it is forgotten
often as they join forces to take on a team from Truro,
who make an annual visit. They also play, spasmodically,
Newlyn Non Athletico, a level 14 English football team.

If any of this rings a bell, then you've got David

Beckham, Steven Gerrard and Jose Mourinho to thank, as they were amongst an invasion of star names who descended on the island to make an Adidas advertisement called 'Dream Big'. You can watch it on the internet if you like.

A sad footnote to a truly romantic tale is that the Isles of Scilly are facing a real battle when it comes to holding on to their young folk. With no sixth-form education, most kids are heading to the mainland at 16, leaving the average age of a player currently standing at around the mid-to-late thirties mark. If it gets much worse, they might have to substitute the half-time oranges for meals-on-wheels.

It's easy to read a tale like this and feel relieved that things are different around your neck of the woods, but take a look at, for example, the Scottish Premier League, and you could be forgiven for thinking that they are in a similar situation. Since Aberdeen roared to glory in 1984/85, it's been all Glasgow, with Rangers and Celtic hoovering up every league crown between them.

If you really want a monopoly, take a gander towards Latvia, and a side called Skonto FC, who joined the newly formed Virsliga in 1994, and promptly won 14 titles in a row. How dull!

Newry City, then Town, is responsible for the career of Northern Ireland's greatest ever servant. Goalie Pat Jennings had opted to play Gaelic Football until, at 16, he was persuaded to play for an injury ridden youth side. Two years later, he was transferred to Watford for £6,500.

At least those in charge of the English top flight have been sensible enough to safeguard against such financial domination by a small, select group of . . . oh. Regardless, let's hope the genuine smallest league in the world continues long into the 21st century and, who knows, maybe one day a third team will enter the fray, allowing the fans to once again bellow out the glorious chant of 'Can we play you every week?!', because right now it doesn't carry any weight.

35. Did We Win? It's in the Banks!

No enforced absence has affected a team quite as much as that of Gordon Banks in 1970.

We all know how the story goes. England were World Champions, and amongst the favourites to lift the World Cup trophy. Then came Montezuma's Revenge, when England surrendered a 2–0 lead to West Germany, brought on by a soft goal allowed by Banks's replacement Peter 'The Cat' Bonetti, who would never be capped by England again.

Banksy had already set Mexico, and the watching world, alight when he pulled off a save that is still regarded as the greatest of all time, diving to his right to keep out a point-blank downward bullet header from Pele. Although England would go on to lose this group game 1–0, they showed that they could match the Brazilians over 90 minutes in all but the 'goals for' column.

His illness two days before the quarter-final was as untimely as it was mysterious. Banks claimed to have

The New Saints FC will always have a special place in Steven Gerrard's heart. In 2005, when they were known as Total Network Solutions, they suffered Stevie's first ever senior hat-trick, in a Champions League qualifier at Anfield.

done nothing different from any other member of the team. Regardless, he was struck down by quite ghastly stomach problems, with unthinkable liquids pouring out of both ends.

Still, the England coaching staff, led by Sir Alf Ramsey, were desperate for him to play, so he was set the most basic of fitness tests on the morning of the game. His challenge? To jog to a nearby tree and back. He obviously managed it, but as his condition deteriorated, Ramsey had no choice but to leave him back in the team hotel, and it is here that the lesser-known part of this otherwise famous story takes place.

Banks's condition was not getting any better, forcing him on to his back and into a horizontal position to watch his team-mates do battle against their biggest enemy. However, this was in the days before round-the-clock coverage, and the game itself wasn't even being shown live in the host country. England's number 1 was actually watching a delayed feed.

An hour into the match, no illness could have suppressed Gordon's grin. 2–0 up against the Germans, a semi-final berth against Italy awaiting, and a genuine chance of reversing their slim defeat against a Brazilian side now regarded as the best there's ever been. Make no mistake, England had already proved that they were the only team in 1970 with the potential to do so.

When he heard the team coach return, Banks bounded out to greet his triumphant team-mates, only to be met with long faces writ large with shattered dreams and, in the case of Bobby Charlton, tears. Gordon returned to his TV to watch the nightmare unfold, more than an hour after the torrid turn of events had actually taken place.

On his return to England, the keeper was ordered to remain at home for a full week while tests were carried out, unsuccessfully, to establish just what had struck him down. Some say he was poisoned, but whatever it was, I'm sure he never felt as sick as he did when he first clapped eyes on his beleaguered England squad trudging into that hotel lobby.

6

Breaking the Law

36. Home-made Footballs and Overthrown Governments

The first FIFA World Cup, in 1930 was, quite literally, a load of old balls, and within it lie countless lesser-spotted football stories, each of them as laughable as the one before.

I originally researched this particular parable because I knew of the astonishing pre-match scandal surrounding the final itself, but in doing so discovered a list of reasons why this tournament could arguably be struck from the record books. So, before I can reach my original point, let me begin at the beginning.

Olympic Champions Uruguay were celebrating their centenary of independence, and were therefore deemed best placed to host the inaugural finals. This threw up one main problem; namely, how in God's great earth were any European teams going to get there?

Originally, eight countries accepted the open invitation to all FIFA affiliates (British sides had withdrawn from the governing body after disputes over payments to

---

Newtown's home ground pays homage to one of Wales's greatest men. Latham Park is named after war hero George Latham, a star for Liverpool and Wales, and the manager who led Cardiff to that landmark FA Cup triumph in 1927.

amateur players), with the furthest flung being ... hold on, let me just check my map ... the USA.

This was simply because any European team would have to pay for a financially unfeasible boat trip across the Atlantic. So desperate were FIFA that they paid for Belgium, France, Romania and Yugoslavia to make the journey.

One member of the Yugoslav side, Lucien Laurent, has since talked of how it took fifteen days, with basic exercises taking place below deck and training on deck. Apparently, not one tactical session was conducted, and they used to get fairly peeved off with the left-back who constantly hoofed the ball 70 yards into Row Z.

So, before a ball was kicked in earnest, four European sides arrived boat-lagged and seasick, with a timetable of preparation more suitable to a team of lobster. And when the games began, controversy reared its head at almost every turn.

Take France versus Argentina in Group A. The Argentinians, with their fanatical support, were struggling to hold on to a 1–0 lead, so Brazilian referee Almeida Rego just blew the whistle early. After half an hour, during which the blue and white stripes were able to get their breath back, he resumed the game for the final six minutes. With momentum, pattern and physical advantage diminished, there were no more goals. All of a sudden, Graham Poll's World Cup career looks much more impressive, although he's destined to be remembered for the three yellow cards he famously dished out to Croatia's Josip Simunic in a Group F encounter with Australia in the 2006 finals.

Back to 1930, and the USA beat Belgium 3–0 in their opening game, although the Belgians were aghast not only at the conditions of the ground and pitch, but at countless refereeing decisions – including a goal that was so offside, the scorer was actually in another time zone. Something tells me that transatlantic opposition was not exactly being welcomed with open arms, which seemed to be borne out in Uruguay's semi-final against Yugoslavia, when the visitors had an equalising goal ruled out by an inexplicable offside decision. Uruguay, by the way, when accused by opposition teams of employing violent on-field tactics, told them publicly to toughen up. Brilliant. So, with Argentina and hosts Uruguay making the final, at least we could forget about those pesky Europeans with their stupid hats and knives and forks, and concentrate on a good, clean final. Of course not. In fact, the controversy surrounding the final is the only reason I'm talking about the 1930 World Cup at all.

Before kick-off, an argument broke out regarding which football to use, given that both sides had brought their own, just like I did when meeting my mates from school down the local park on a Sunday. Now, you would assume that this situation would have been resolved before the tournament began. This type of disorganisation throws up some obvious questions. Firstly, was Sepp Blatter

---

Northampton Town's more frugal fans avoid paying into the impressive Sixfields Stadium by gathering on a nearby hill which offers a view of the pitch, albeit only one part of it – meaning, for them, it really is a game of two halves.

already in charge of FIFA at this time? And secondly, who chose the footballs for the earlier games? Something tells me that those visiting European sides had little say in the matter.

Now, it is important to point out that these balls differed greatly, given that they were hand-made by representatives of each side, rather than bought in a shop or approved by FIFA. Goodness no, that would be too, I don't know, not completely ridiculous!

It was decided by FIFA that the Argentinian footie would be used for the first half, and the Uruguayan ball in the all-important second half. Nowhere can I find exact details of the specifications of each football, but it's likely that Uruguay used a Tiento: a rubber bladder, which would be inserted into a leather casing and tied up with 'tiento' – a leather cord. Accounts of its total weight vary depending on which story you believe, with some saying it weighed around four stone, and others claiming closer to six. It was not uncommon for play to be stopped during a game in order that an official could grab a pump and reflate the ball, as the security valve had not yet been invented. This particular type of ball would also deform during the course of a match due to the loose bladder.

Argentina, who were much fancied heading into the game, trotted off to the dressing room at half time in control and 2–1 up. Cue Tiento, and a full-time score of 4–2 in favour of Uruguay, with the winning goal scored by Hector Castro, who had only one hand after losing the other in a childhood accident. Given that this encounter was played out on a snow-covered pitch, one can only predict said football was comparable to a ten-pin bowling ball.

The remarkable story of the first ever World Cup didn't end at the final whistle either, with the victorious players being awarded some land and a fancy house by the government in Montevideo.

Meanwhile, the shock of Argentina's defeat was such that rioting in the streets turned into a military coup, and President Irigoyen was overthrown just three days later.

Now, taking into account all of the above factors that came together to define the first World Cup, you might be forgiven for condemning the inaugural Greatest Show on Earth. But I couldn't disagree more. Bent referees? Footballs that favoured one team over another? Violent tactics? The only real thing that's changed is the travel arrangements.

37. Hello, Is It Me You're Looking For?

As Graeme Souness headed for the Southampton dressing room at full time of a home defeat by Leeds United, he could have been forgiven for thinking that Jeremy Beadle was about to jump out of a locker.

In 1996 the Scotsman fell foul of the domestic game's biggest and funniest ever hoax, which all began with an unexpected phone call.

The voice on the other end of the line introduced himself as none other than AC Milan's World Player of the Year, George Weah. He had taken time out of his busy schedule to inform the Saints boss of a unique opportunity to snap up his talented cousin, Ali Dia. Why he would even bother to do this in the first place is a question for Mr Souness, not me.

Ali had been capped by his native Senegal and played club football for Paris Saint-Germain, or so the caller said, and he would be a true star if given the chance to prove himself in the best league in the world.

Not one to pass on a golden opportunity, Souness invited Dia for a trial. Most of the other players have since commented on how bad he was during that five-a-side game, so Souness baffled almost everyone at the club by awarding him a one-month contract. Not only that, but he drafted him straight into the squad for a home game the very next day against Leeds United.

Ali Dia made his big entrance in the 32nd minute following an injury to Matthew Le Tissier, and what transpired over the course of 21 fleeting minutes will go down as one of the most cringe-worthy, embarrassing and downright hilarious episodes ever to grace English football.

With the running style of Forrest Gump, the first touch of Mike Tyson and the overall ability of an inanimate steel rod, so bad was Dia's performance that the substitute had to be substituted himself shortly after the restart.

Le Tiss remembers it well: 'Trialists used to come and go and we thought we'd never see this guy again. Then we turned up for the game against Leeds the following day and he was named on the subs bench, and we thought "this is a bit strange".'

And as for his performance on the pitch?

'He ran around the pitch like Bambi on ice. It was very, very embarrassing to watch. I don't think he realised what position he was supposed to be in.'

How could George Weah have got it so terribly wrong? Was he blinded by family loyalty? Or was Ali Dia actually the future of Southampton and they just didn't give him

---

Norwich City is the only English side to ever beat Bayern Munich at their Olympic Stadium. Their 2–1 win in the 1993/94 UEFA Cup sent shockwaves through football. Bayern have since moved to the Allienz Arena, thus cementing this record in history.

enough opportunity to adapt to the English game?

The answer is none of the above, because it wasn't Weah on the phone to Souness in the first place, but instead Dia's agent.

The Scotsman bought it hook, line and sinker, only to come a cropper in front of the mocking eyes of millions of fans.

Ali Dia was not George Weah's cousin, nor had he played for European heavyweights PSG. Instead, he'd pottered around in the German and French lower leagues and had already been rejected after trials at Port Vale, Gillingham and Portsmouth.

To add insult to injury, West Ham boss Harry Redknapp confirmed that he had received the exact same phone call but had dismissed it out of hand.

Ali would go on to play for non-league Gateshead, albeit briefly, after enduring endless chants of 'A-Li Dia, Is a Liar, Is a Liar'. Repeat until out of breath.

This is, by far, the best example of a club being duped, but other hoaxes have enjoyed phenomenal success at the expense of the newspaper industry.

In 1999 the *News of the World* printed a story linking Liverpool and Arsenal to a promising young Frenchman called Didier Baptiste.

The scoop was true in terms of the player's nationality and the fact that he was a left-back, but what the paper failed to realise was that the footballer in question was a fictional character from Sky One's sporting soap opera *Dream Team*.

He didn't play for AS Monaco and the French Under-21 side, but instead for the fictional Harchester Rovers.

It was a bit like claiming *Coronation Street*'s Bet Lynch was in the running for the Chelsea manager's job.

The story, released by a practical joker at a news agency, went unchecked, and was printed as gospel by the paper, only for *The Times* and the *Observer* to astonishingly run follow-up pieces the next day.

Tom Redhill, who played the part of Baptiste on telly, must have choked on his toast when he picked up the sports section that morning and found out that two Premier League clubs were in a tug of war for his estimated £3.5m signature.

This story has been twisted over the years, with some fans actually believing that Gerard Houllier and Arsene Wenger had been conned into bidding for a television character, but it was the media who fell for the prank, not the clubs themselves.

As technology improves and people become more internet savvy, the online hoax appears to be all but dead, although hope reared its head in January 2009 when *The Times* printed its list of Football's Top 50 Rising Stars.

Hidden amongst the Dan Goslings and Karim Benzemas of this world was Masal Bugdov, described in the article as 'Moldova's finest . . .'

The piece went on to claim that 'The 16-year-old

Nottingham Forest was the first side to attach nets to a goal frame, and played the first recorded match where a referee used a whistle. And, in 1894, when captain Sam Weller Widdowson stuffed adapted cricket pads down his socks, the shin pad was born.

attacker has been strongly linked with a move to Arsenal, work permit permitting. And he's been linked with plenty of other top clubs as well.'

As you've probably guessed, there was no such player; an internet prankster had created an entire back story based around a phantom boy wonder.

Given this new success, I might have a go myself, spreading a rumour that Craig Bellamy is worth £14m. Surely, no one will swallow that.

38. I'll Have a Fiver Witch-Way Please . . .

Double, double, my bet's in trouble, then Laursen scores and Barry doubles . . . Okay, so I am no Shakespeare, but I do wish that I could turn my Saturday bet from a loser to a winner by merely casting a spell, rubbing a lucky charm or sticking a well-placed pin into a voodoo doll of Gary Neville, the latter of which I have actually tried.

Picture the scene. It's 4.43 p.m. on a Saturday afternoon, and Jeff Stelling has just delivered news of a late strike that has turned my slip into toilet paper. I calmly reach down the side of my armchair, grab the chicken I have been saving for such an occasion, and issue it with its last cluck. Five minutes later and two late goals from my chosen team, I'm a rich man.

Obviously, I'm either hallucinating whilst writing this book or there is a point to such ludicrous fiction.

Superstition, rituals and witchcraft have affected football since the first ball was kicked – from the inane to the quite grotesque. While some have tried to bribe referees, others have instead turned to the supernatural.

Seeing as I have already killed a chicken, let's start in Turkey, and a story involving Sir Les Ferdinand, who joined Besiktas on loan from QPR in 1988.

The striker may have wondered why 35,000 people had

turned up to watch his first training session, but all would be revealed in quite gory fashion.

Before Ferdinand was able to attempt a volley in earnest, a club official dragged a lamb on to the pitch, where he proceeded to sacrifice it, then scooped up its blood and smeared it on to our Les's forehead and boots. Welcome to Turkey, Mr Ferdinand.

This gruesome tradition has been relayed by other English professionals who have turned out for a club in this region. In Dean Saunders's case, at Galatasaray, it was a sheep, but at least they had the decency to slaughter it in the privacy of their own dressing room.

You might think that this type of tomfoolery is a dying art, but during the 2008 African Cup of Nations the Egyptian squad called a halt to a training session in order to – how can I put this? – kill a cow. Maybe former Wigan forward Amr Zaki, a member of that side, should have suggested the idea to his manager Steve Bruce, in order to bring the boys together. Egypt, by the way, won the 2008 African Cup of Nations, but don't even dare contemplate that 'the cow did it'! On second thoughts . . .

As a Northern Ireland supporter, I think it's time for desperate measures. We haven't qualified for a major tournament since 1986, and if all it takes is for me to bound up to Nigel Worthington and rub a hamster in his face, then that's what I'm going to have to darn well do. But no . . . for every coincidence there is a story that dispels the notion that there is any merit in the witchcraft style of management.

Before the 2006 World Cup, Togo's chief voodoo priest, Togbui Assiogbo Gnagblondjro III, talked to the ancestral spirits and declared that his country would go 'far at the World Cup'. He was nearly right. They got thumped by Korea, France and Switzerland, scoring only one goal in their three straight defeats. Nice work Togbui; have you got a business card?

It's not just these goings-on in African football, but more the day-to-day delusions, that bewilder.

One game in particular stands out, when two of Tanzania's leading teams, Simba and Yanga, went so crazy with pre-match antics that both clubs were fined by their governing body.

It began when Simba players sprinkled a 'mystical' powder around their penalty box, while, at the same time, their goalkeeper took the liberty of breaking eggs on to his goalposts. Two Yanga players retaliated by urinating on the pitch, not because the toilets were out of order, but because this was meant to cancel out the talc and the yolks. They can both claim success, given that the game ended in a 2–2 draw.

Maybe Barry Fry was in the stands that day, because he repeated almost the same trick, only this time it wasn't in deepest Tanzania, but in Birmingham.

He had just been given the manager's job at City when he was regaled with the story of a curse that had been put on the St Andrews pitch by a disgruntled old gypsy lady.

Notts County is the ultimate yo-yo club, having been promoted 12 times and relegated on 15 occasions since forming in 1862, which also makes them the oldest remaining fully professional club in the league.

Barry, convinced of its authenticity, employed a medium to gauge the vibe of the pitch, only to be given some rather bladder-busting advice.

Despite not being young of age, he was told to wait until the exact stroke of midnight on the eve of his next home fixture, and, as the chimes rang out, to pee in all four corners of the playing surface, in order to lift the hex.

Instead of turning said crackpot on her heels and sending her back to the psychiatric ward from which she came, he carried out her orders to the letter.

At five to three the following afternoon he strolled to the dugout in confident mood, which lasted all of about 15 minutes, as Wolverhampton Wanderers banged in four without reply. Goodness help anyone who slipped whilst taking a corner kick.

It's with regret that I have to inform you of one more urine-related story.

It centres around Argentina goalie Sergio Goycochea, who felt the call of nature just before his country's 1990 World Cup quarter-final penalty showdown against Yugoslavia. Despite the 349 cameras, carrying the game live to 2,385 nations worldwide, he 'discreetly' popped it out and relieved himself beside his goalmouth.

Argentina won the shoot-out, only to find themselves once again facing the spot-kick showdown in the semi-final against Italy. Fear not, Captain Urinal is here! Good old Goycochea re-enacted his 'lucky charm' and, before you could say Splash-back, they'd progressed.

Maybe Sergio should have spent a quick penny before Andreas Brehme scored the winning penalty for West Germany in the final.

Another bizarre ritual of circumstance came about after Don Revie's Leeds United side of the 1960s were forced to walk the last two miles to a match after being stuck in horrendous traffic. As they picked up the away win, Revie then forced his players to run the gauntlet of opposition support by making them repeat the feat for several away games thereafter. Big Don, of course, was also the man who wore the same blue shirt on match days for over a decade.

And that brings us rather nicely on to the quirks and eccentricities of players themselves, from the vintage to the bang up-to-date.

None other than Chelsea and England's John Terry is famous for his idiosyncrasies, which include always sitting on the same team coach seat, listening to the same music in his car on the way to training (Usher, if you must know), parking in the same space and using the same urinal in the home dressing room. And that's not all . . .

JT wore the same 'lucky' shin pads for an entire decade, only to lose them after throwing them to the side of the pitch in the closing minutes of a 2004 Champions League defeat to Barcelona at the Nou Camp. He was virtually inconsolable.

I am sure Mr Terry is a bright young chap, who

Oldham Athletics' four nearest rivals – Bury, Manchester United, Manchester City and Rochdale – are all within nine miles of Boundary Park, but none of them is in the same division as the Latics, forcing the club to look further afield for derby days.

undoubtedly has a great mind for football, but his quote in the *Mirror* beggars belief: 'Those shin pads had got me to where I was in the game – and I'd lost them. I really felt terrible because they were a big part of my routine.

'Before the [Carling Cup] final I was having a go at the kitman even though it wasn't his fault. I was thinking . . . I've had those shin pads for so long and now this is it, all over.'

This temporary bout of brain-freeze can be matched only by then French boss Raymond Domenech, or can it? He had allegedly said, ahead of the 2006 World Cup finals, that he didn't trust Scorpios. Some bright spark sourced the star signs of his entire squad and found not one single player born between 16 November and 15 December. Strange, but not exactly admissible in court.

From AC Milan midfielder Gennaro Gattuso reading Dostoyevsky aloud in the changing room before every game, to Adrian Mutu wearing his pants inside out (fat lot of good that did him at Chelsea!), the game is still riddled with crackpot habits. And they've learned from the best.

Holland's mercurial Johan Cruyff was riddled with ritual, from slapping his goalkeeper in the stomach to spitting his chewing gum into the opposition half just before kick-off.

Before you start laughing at those crazy foreigners, you'd be best advised to save it.

Gary Lineker, the level-headed voice of football, never shot at goal during pre-match warm-ups because he believed it would reduce his chances of scoring during the game.

Whether it's Laurent Blanc planting a wet one on Fabian Barthez's noggin, or Bobby Moore refusing to put his shorts on before the rest of the England team, there are no limits to the depths of stupidity a footballer can plumb when he truly believes in pointless superstition.

Why do they do it? One story, featuring none other than Pele himself, gives us the answer.

After giving his jersey away to a fan at the end of a game, the wizard lost his magic. Well, he didn't actually, he just suffered a bad run of form. He convinced himself that this dip was a direct result of his change of top, so he begged a friend to retrieve the garment. A week later his pal handed over Pele's recaptured lucky jersey, and he immediately regained his touch.

However, it later transpired that his friend had not been able to track down the shirt he'd lost and had instead just given the great man back the same one Pele had worn throughout his entire bad spell.

Proof, if needed, that such superstitions are all in the mind, otherwise I'd have a horseshoe on my belt loop, a rabbit's foot down my sock, a wishbone for a bracelet and a four-leaf clover in my hair, just as I smashed home the winning goal in the 2012 World Cup final for Northern Ireland, running straight to the bench to embrace Nigel Worthington's bloodied face.

39. When the Reds Go Marching ... Off

Just like Saint Gary Lineker, I can proudly claim to have never been red carded in my entire footballing career.

Having said that, the difference between the silver fox and myself is that I rarely performed well enough to be picked for any side, whether at school or during various amateur tournaments I've played in.

On one occasion I was brought on as a second-half substitute for a BBC Radio 1 side during a quarter-final match at a pro-celeb event at Reading's Madejski Stadium. My first contribution was to scythe down a still sprightly Mark Bright, catching him round about the knee. Clutching a newly formed bruise, he looked up from the ground and informed me in no uncertain terms what type of person he thought I was when I found myself alone in bed at night. Still, I only saw yellow.

One red card can change an entire game, sometimes for the better, sometimes for the worse, and repeat offenders stick out like a sore shin in the history books.

The Premier League record is jointly held by big Duncan Ferguson and Patrick Viera, both red carded a bone-crushingly staggering eight times. Vinnie Jones, Roy Keane and Alan Smith are just one flash of *rouge* behind them, while the likes of John Hartson and Eric Cantona all feature in the rogues' top ten, but you could have probably guessed that.

Less obvious are those individual games that produced the most early showers in history. Forget British clubs, and instead observe two Paraguayan sides who turned a football field into one big boxing ring.

The clash between Sportivo Ameliano and General Caballero was already heated after a hotly disputed red card was brandished to a Sportivo player. When a second one appeared, tensions not only boiled over, but positively exploded, with almost every man left on the pitch indulging in a Wild-West style brawl that would have left Clint Eastwood himself cowering behind an advertising hoarding.

For a full ten minutes, both sides punched holes in each other, leaving several in need of bandages, stitches and nose realignment. When order was finally restored, the referee, playing it by the book, sent off a further 18 offenders in one fell swoop, leaving just two righteous souls eligible to continue. The match was abandoned.

In 2009, however, in similar circumstances a Spanish referee attracted the attention of Norris McWhirter's replacement, banishing 19 players during a second tier game between Recreativo Linense and Saladillo de Algeciras. Anarchy reigned after he dismissed a player for

---

Peterborough United hold the record for the most goals scored in a single season by any English club. They filled the onion bag 134 times in their 1960/61 campaign, with Terry Bly scoring 52 of them, still an all-time club best.

a foul, but he consequently sent off nine members of each team after the furore, and members of the crowd as well, so bonus points there.

An honourable mention must go to the infamous and almost always misinterpreted Football War between El Salvador and Honduras in 1969.

Legend has it that a World Cup qualifying play-off between the two teams led to a four-day war between the nations, but the real truth is that the match happened to coincide with an explosion of tension between the neighbouring countries and, in some ways, was used by those in high places as a vehicle to express hatred.

On 27 June El Salvador outshot their bitter rivals on the field by three goals to two, while the first shots were fired off the field on 14 July, but there is no doubt that the sporting clash accelerated both nations' journey up the path to inevitable bloody confrontation, with claims and counter claims being made about on-field cheating and off-field kidnappings and violence.

Back in Blighty, we can't compete with such war and barbarity, the British record being a paltry five, which randomly happened twice in 1997, although in separate seasons.

In February a Plymouth Argyle player was sent off for a two-footed challenge on Bruce Grobbelaar, with the ensuing dust-up leading to further dismissals.

It was much the same story when Wigan travelled to Bristol Rovers in December, with four red cards appearing before the half-time whistle, and another for a separate incident after the break.

So, I'm afraid, when it comes to fists, we can't match

the rest of the world, despite hard men like Vinnie and Duncan, and my barbaric chopping down of Mark Bright.

We can, however, pay homage to Dundee's Andy McLaren who holds the dubious record of being sent off three times in one match.

First given his marching orders for smacking a counterpart, he then struck out again as he left the pitch, prompting the ref to once again flash the card. Undeterred, Mr McLaren marched straight down the tunnel and proceeded to boot in the door of the official's locker, earning him a belated third reprimand. He never played for Dundee again.

We can also claim responsibility for the mere existence of yellow and red cards, as it was a British referee called Ken Aston who came up with the idea. It was first implemented in the 1970 World Cup in Mexico, which ironically produced not one sending-off.

I'll leave this subject via the story of what has to be the most bizarre red card of all time.

It came about during an amateur game between Hatfield and Hertford Heath in Hertfordshire, when referee Gary Bailey sent off a nine-year-old called Me-Tu, for repeatedly calling the players Pretty Boy. Not that strange, I hear you say, but it is when you take into account

---

Plymouth Argyle fans travel ridiculous distances to follow their team. The Green Army's nearest game, against Bristol City, is 116 miles away, with furthest flung Norwich City involving a 716-mile round trip. They are the most southern *and* most western league side in Britain.

that Me-Tu was actually a Senegalese parrot. The tropical pest was also mimicking the noise of the ref's whistle, causing players to stop mid-game.

Me-Tu was perched on the shoulder of 66-year-old Irene Kerrigan, who often brought her pet along to enjoy an afternoon encounter. I'm not sure what's more ludicrous: bringing a parrot to a football match or a referee physically sending it off.

40. Match of the Uday

Everyone is entitled to their own opinion, but when it comes to grabbing a game by the scruff of the neck and directly influencing the outcome, there's one to beat them all.

There have been hundreds of special footballers, but to have the ability to physically determine the final result is a rare skill. Some say Maradona, others say Gerrard, but my favourite dictator has to be Saddam Hussein.

Lack of democracy in a country usually leads to interference on the field of play from the very highest echelons of power, something experienced first hand by my good friend Pat Nevin, who played for Chelsea against Iraq in 1986.

When the nippy Scotsman first touched on this anecdote during an episode of BBC Radio Five Live's *Fighting Talk*, which I host every Saturday morning (have I mentioned that?), I naturally assumed he was making it up for laughs. Not so. I was delighted when he agreed to tell the full tale of 'When Pat (Nearly) Met Saddam' for this book.

Iraq had qualified for the World Cup and, somehow, Chelsea found themselves in Baghdad for a warm-up game. Remember, at this time, Saddam was our friend. In the immortal words of Bill Hicks, 'check the receipts'.

'It was just another Middle Eastern country at the time, although I thought it slightly odd that we weren't allowed to fly directly into Baghdad. Instead we landed in Jordan and were bussed from there.

'Most of the squad just lounged around the hotel for a few days before the game, but I took one of the lads, John Miller, to explore the city. We had limousines at our beck and call, but when we got out and walked around the city, we were followed by four members of the secret police.

'We tried to dress down but, on hindsight, we looked like a couple of extras from a Duran Duran video. I remember on every street corner there was a gun-toting member of the Ba'ath Party, all in fatigues, all wearing shades, but it's worth noting we never once felt in danger, apart from when I nearly ate a dodgy bowl of stew with a boar's head in it.'

So, how come Saddam Hussein changed the result of a football match between Chelsea and Iraq?

'We arrived at the ground and it was heaving. The stands were chock-a-block, although the entire pitch was ringed by the Republican Guard.

'We ran out to a warm reception, and took our places ready for kick-off, but nothing happened. We were there, the Iraqi national side were there, and the referee was in place, but nothing happened.'

Despite this random occurrence of two sides just standing around in sweltering heat, no words of concern or objection were voiced and, after about an hour, events took a peculiar turn.

'All of a sudden, the entire stadium went down on their knees, presumably in prayer or worship. Not knowing what to do, we all decided to sit on the dirt pitch in a circle.'

Once the devotions ended, the match began, and what took place on the field was actually quite exciting. Iraq opened the scoring with a belter of a strike from outside the area, but Chelsea eventually strolled their way to an equaliser, and the game ended in a respectable 1–1 draw. However, that doesn't explain the delay, which brought about a heavy case of sunburn on the face of the pint-sized winger they call Pat Nevin.

'It transpired that the match couldn't start until Saddam Hussein turned up, and he was running late, so two teams, the officials, and 20,000 fans had to wait for him to arrive at the ground.'

Then, post full time, came a moment that pricked Pat's curiosity.

'We went up to collect medals of some sort, only we received them from his son Uday. Despite us waiting an hour for him, Saddam couldn't wait an extra two minutes for us!'

This is the same Uday Hussein who used to keep notes on players' performances in order to determine how many times the soles of a player's feet should be whipped as brutal punishment after a defeat.

'After we were given our trinkets, the Iraq team climbed

Porthmadog striker David Taylor picked up the prestigious European Golden Boot in the 1993/94 season, pipping the great and the good with 43 goals and, in doing so, denying Glasgow Rangers' Ally McCoist three-in-a-row.

the stairs and hoisted aloft the biggest trophy I have ever seen. You would never have guessed the game finished all even.'

That's because, in the eyes of the Iraqi nation, it didn't.

'The next morning, as we left the hotel for our flight home, I decided to grab the local, state-run newspaper and lo and behold, there was the story of how Iraq had beaten Chelsea 2–1.'

Saddam, it seemed, had metaphorically popped up in injury time to score a late winner. Predictable, I suppose, but why were Chelsea playing this ridiculous warm-up game in the first place? The mind boggles.

I could fill an entire book about politics in football, but staying strictly with dictators, most of them have matched their passion for brutality with a fondness for football.

The most famous instance came in 1938, just before the outbreak of the Second World War, when England travelled to Berlin to face Germany.

After strong persuasion by the British ambassador, the visiting side, including a young Stanley Matthews, gave a Nazi salute during a rousing rendition of the German national anthem.

Adolf Hitler, who didn't take kindly to the mention of balls, had more important things to do that day than watch a footie match, but in amongst the 100,000-strong crowd were Hermann Goering and Joseph Goebbels, both of whom were crying into their Bovril as England hammered the home team 6–3.

Just four years previously, Benito Mussolini made sure that the second ever World Cup, held in his native Italy, was almost as much a farce as the first one which is detailed elsewhere in this book.

For the Fascist Party leader the tournament was a propaganda tool, and the laws of the game were worth less than the paper they were printed on.

Italy fielded ringers (three Argentinians who suddenly claimed to have Italian ancestry), employed on-field tactics more suited to ice hockey, and made sure the referees turned a blind eye to the whole shameful affair.

I should probably use the word 'allegedly', but a BBC documentary confirmed that two officials, after overseeing Italy games, were suspended by their own associations following the finals.

My favourite official is Swede Ivan Eklind, who actually met with Mussolini prior to Italy's 1–0 semi-final win against Austria. One story suggests that, during the game, he headed the ball to a blue shirt!

It was little wonder he returned to officiate the final. Full-time score? Benito Mussolini 2, Czechoslovakia 1.

No tyrant has influenced the history of football more than General Franco, a Real Madrid fanatic, who helped them secure the services of one of the finest players of all time.

Argentinian Alfredo di Stefano was plying his trade at

Portsmouth has broken its club record transfer fee twice on the same player. They signed Peter Crouch from QPR in 2001 for £1.5 million, then repeated the feat in 2008, paying Liverpool £11 million for him to return to Fratton Park for a second stint.

Millionarios in Colombia, but quickly became a target for Barcelona.

In 1953 the deal broker was a lawyer called Roman Trias Gargas, who would later claim that his phone had been bugged by Real Madrid.

A deal was done but, at the 11th hour, Barca president Marti Carreto refused to rubber stamp it, leading to accusations that pressure had been placed on him from Real Madrid, with the blessing of Franco. Some have alleged that threats to his well-being had been made; the real reason for his inexplicable change of heart.

Alfredo di Stefano eventually joined Real Madrid, and scored in all five of their consecutive European Cup final victories between 1956 and 1960.

In 1973 the great Johan Cruyff made it clear that he could never join Real because of their association with Franco.

This, by the way, is the same despot who withdrew the Spanish national side from the first ever European Championships in 1960, because they were due to play the USSR in the quarter-finals, and he was peeved at them for opposing him during the Spanish Civil War over two decades previously.

As recently as 1978, dictators have found it impossible to sit in their heavily fortified palaces and leave football to the people. Argentina won the World Cup that year, but allegations of bribery have circulated ever since.

At the centre of it all was General Videla, a vile creature who oversaw the 'disappearance' of approximately 30,000 of his own citizens.

In their second group phase match – effectively a semi-final – the home side needed to beat Peru by four clear goals in order to qualify for the ultimate showcase. Under a cloud of bribery allegations, they eased their way to a 6–0 final scoreline against a Peru side who hardly broke a sweat.

Some say it was because the Peruvians had already been eliminated, while many point to the shadowy figure of General Videla.

If, in the future, Britain becomes an autocracy, the first point of order should be to determine our new leader's footballing allegiance. I'll be buying a season ticket for his or her chosen team almost immediately.

41. Shoot! No, Don't! Yes, Do! I Need to Lie Down

The beauty of football lies in its simplicity.

When Ebenezer Cobb Morley first drew up the initial rules in 1863 there were only 13 points, 12 of which still form the backbone of the game today, the exception being 'no player shall run with the ball', although Jimmy Floyd Hasselbaink has done his best to honour all thirteen.

Even today, with FIFA's 138-page document of updated rules, available for all incurable insomniacs to peruse on their website, it remains a simple game to understand, with the only real sticking point being the explanation to fair-weather fans of the offside rule but, hey, that's what salt and pepper shakers are for.

I mean, in how many sports can you actually explain all its vital elements in less than a hundred words? Here goes . . .

The aim is to score by hitting ball into the opposition goal. The goalkeepers are the only players allowed to use hands to move the ball in open play; the rest of the team use their feet, or any part of their torso apart from their arms.

The team that scores the most goals wins. If it's tied, extra time and/or penalties are played. There are eleven players on each side, with two halves of 45 minutes forming a regulation

*game. Don't kick a player before the ball. Complain about
every decision. For offside rule, see salt and pepper.*

There you go, 99 words, for the basic rules of football.
Despite how easy it is to understand, those in charge see
fit to constantly tamper, hence the pointless telephone
book of laws that now exist. For the most part, they have
little effect, with the obvious exception being the offside
rule, which, on last reading, goes something like this:

'A player is offside when he is the closest player to the
opposition goalkeeper unless he is a) not interfering with
play, b) born in a town beginning with the letter M, c)
able to name at least three members of the A-Team, or
d) knows all the words to "Bohemian Rhapsody".'

Well, it's something like that, anyway. The whole golden
goal fiasco was another embarrassment in 1996,
compounded by the introduction of the silver goal six
years later, both aimed at forcing teams to attack in extra
time, rather than playing for penalties.

While a golden goal killed off a game, a silver goal meant
that you still had to see out the applicable 15-minute
period of extra time, giving the other team a short-lived
opportunity to throw the kitchen sink at you.

Only one team, Greece, ever scored a silver goal, namely
in the semi-final of Euro 2002, earning them a place in

Port Talbot Town, despite having a population of around
35,000, has developed a senior and youth system that sees
no fewer than 17 teams playing outside of their first string,
the youngest being an Under-Seven side.

the final at the expense of the Czech Republic. These equally ludicrous inventions were binned shortly after this game, and a return to the original 'fifteen minutes each way' was heralded.

Proof that, even when presented with a straightforward game of football, those in suits cannot stop themselves interfering. Alarmingly, we don't often hear about it, as FIFA target part-time and amateur leagues to test out their odd-ball theories.

In 1991 the Isthmian League (now Ryman's) was mysteriously ordered to replace the common 'throw-in' with a 'kick-in'. Any person who has ever played football will tell you exactly what the outcome will be, specifically that sides will tell their centre-backs to get into the box and they'll continually hoof the ball into the penalty area for an anticipated long-ball dogfight. And that's precisely what happened, although half the teams refused to take part and continued to throw the ball into play; good on them.

It was a quite bizarre and pointless change of procedure, beaten only by the story of the 1993/94 Shell Caribbean Cup, when an innocuous rule would lead to, possibly, the most farcical game of football since old Ebenezer the Geezer first put pen to paper.

The tournament is this region's answer to the Copa America, or the European Championships, with every island in the area taking part.

Barbados were playing Grenada in the final match of Group A, needing to win by two clear goals to go through to the next stage on superior goal difference.

Everything was going according to plan, with the

Barbadians scoring twice without reply until, that is, the 83rd minute, when Grenada pulled a goal back. Enter the strangest rule in the history of football.

Some bright spark has decided that, in the event of a game going to extra time, a golden-goal style system would be activated and, to encourage teams to seek the win, any team victorious in extra time would be awarded the equivalent of a two-goal victory.

With Grenada now guaranteed qualification with the score at 2–1, they put every man behind the ball immediately from the restart. Barbados, knowing the chances of scoring again in the last five minutes were slim to none, cottoned on that, in levelling the scores at two-each, they could take the game to extra time and, if successful, they'd be awarded the equivalent of a suitable 4–2 win.

So, right on cue, they simply walked the ball into their own net, tying the game and causing widespread confusion across the Caribbean, where the game was being broadcast live. However, it doesn't stop there!

Grenada now realised what was going on, and worked out that if they scored an own goal they would lose three-two and qualify for the next round, so from the resulting kick-off they tried to put the ball into their own net, but

---

Prestatyn Town faced local objections to the installation of floodlights, and was finally only given the go ahead in 2008, but with strict guidelines. Local council ordered that they should be illuminated no later than 9.15 p.m., and only for 12 matches a year.

Barbados had also figured this out. Therefore, for the closing minutes of the game, the most dramatic role reversal in the history of football took place, with Grenada trying to score past their own goalkeeper. This left the Barbados players to defend their opposition's goal, while at the same time trying to thwart Grenada scoring a winner. Are you following me? I know it's complicated but I have genuinely explained it in as simple terms as possible. You may have to read it again.

Alas, Grenada failed to score at either end, which took the game into extra time where, you've guessed it, Barbados fired in the sudden-death strike, giving them the two-goal win they needed.

Barbados went through, Grenada went home. It has to be the most embarrassing game of football ever played, comfortably topping the infamous 'Anschluss match' between Germany and Austria in their final group tie of the 1982 World Cup.

A German win by less than two goals would put both sides through to the next stage at the expense of Algeria. How did they know this? Well, because the Algerians had already played their final group game earlier that day.

After an early German goal by Horst Hrubesch, both sides simply stopped playing proper football, resulting in the most boring and sickening non-event in the history of the game.

Both comrades progressed, but it led to a change in law, so that thereafter all final group clashes had to kick off at the same time. Just what we need, eh? More rules.

42. Bolivia ... Where Cheating Comes Naturally

One problem with playing footie down the park with your mates is a natural inability to run at any reasonable pace after about seven minutes, due to respiratory problems.

This can be caused by one or a combination of the following scenarios: smoking, the common hangover, last night's curry, age, being fat.

Therefore, it's easy to underestimate the level of fitness of professional footballers at the top level. Yes, it's not as hard as working down the mines, but it still takes real discipline and dedication to be able to run for 90 minutes, twice a week, for up to 40 weeks a year, in all sorts of conditions. Obviously, I exclude Dimitar Berbatov from this praise.

It seems that the best of the best can overcome just about everything, from the beating sun to the driving rain, but there's a particular weapon in Mother Nature's armoury that no player can truly conquer, and one team in particular has used this factor to their advantage for close to 100 years.

Bolivia's national football side, on paper, are one of the weakest in world football, yet they have managed to qualify for three World Cups. They also captured the Copa

America against Pele's Brazil in 1963. How, pray tell, did they manage such a feat?

Let me present to you one Osvaldo Cesar Ardiles, a World Cup winner with Argentina in 1978, capped 53 times in total, and somewhat of a cult hero for Spurs, both as player and manager. He's a friend of a friend and has rather kindly honoured this book with a story that explains just exactly why such a rubbish team could become champions of an entire continent.

'On the way to La Paz, the manager's instructions were simple – "Pass, pass, pass ... keep the ball", because losing possession and chasing the ball was far from ideal in the rarefied conditions.

'Also, each attack would involve just two or three players, because when the move broke down the team had no option but to forget about them for a couple of minutes, as it was physically impossible to retreat immediately and resume defensive responsibilities.'

La Paz, you see, is the world's highest capital city, situated at roughly 3,600 metres – that's more than two miles – above sea level. Put simply, unless you're a native, it's pretty hard to breathe there, let alone play football. Breathing – and I don't think I'm overstating the point here – is an essential ingredient when it comes to sporting activities or, let me think, staying alive.

So, not even the deafening roar of Hampden Park on a cold December night or the intimidating chants of the Tifosi in the San Siro can quite compete with the home advantage held by Bolivia. Here's the cold, hard evidence.

In 23 times of asking, they've reached the final of the Copa America only twice, which corresponds nicely with the only two years they've hosted the tournament. As winners in 1963, they stuck five past Brazil and three past Argentina. On the one other occasion, they were breath-taxingly beaten in the final.

Ossie can relate to this, and offers a cautionary tale to any professional footballer who might underestimate the climate issue connected with playing in La Paz. The subject is Ricardo Pizzarotti, a member of Argentina's coaching staff, who told Ardiles and his team-mates on the journey to Bolivia to forget any notion of altitude problems. He insisted that all talk of climate-induced difficulties was complete nonsense.

'Altitude? What altitude?' he bellowed. 'Lack of oxygen? Whatever. Deal with it,' he brashly exclaimed.

He decided to take the lead, stepping off the plane first. He turned back to his squad, took a deliberately deep breath, as if to prove his point, and promptly collapsed. 'They took him away in an ambulance and we didn't see him for a while,' Ossie remembers.

After such a wonderful story, let me hit you with the boring stuff in as short a space as possible. As altitude increases, pressure decreases, so less oxygen is available. It creates two very different sporting environments. In explosive events, such as cycle sprints or short-distance

---

Preston North End holds many 'firsts', including doing the double in the inaugural league season in 1888/89. The team also went through that entire campaign unbeaten, and it would take 115 years before Arsenal matched their vintage invincibles.

running, athletes can perform slightly better, hence the ruling by the athletics' governing body (IAAF) that prevents athletes from officially breaking world records if the event takes place at 1,000 metres or more above sea level.

In sports, such as football, that require stamina over a longer period of time, the reduction in oxygen reduces the athlete's performance. The only way to combat this is to acclimatise, which Ossie and any national team heading to Bolivia do not have time to do. Still awake? Good, let's get back to the footie.

The comparison between Bolivia's home and away record in World Cup qualifiers beggars belief. To date, they have only ever won *three* games away from home, the last being a 7–1 thumping of whipping boys Venezuela in July 1993. Since then they have played 34 *away* qualifiers without a single win. At home, in the very same groups, they've beaten Brazil twice.

Now, it seems more than sensible that FIFA chose to investigate this issue. While it's not the Bolivian people's fault that their country sits at such high altitude, there's a case to be made when it comes to the notion of unfair advantage.

In 2007 FIFA banned any games being played at 2,500 metres or more above sea level. In doing so, Sepp Blatter caused more outrage than if he had walked straight up to the gates of Bolivian President Evo Morales's palace and bared his backside.

Morales called it 'Soccer Apartheid', while Diego Maradona played a charity game in La Paz in support of the lifting of the ban, which by then had already been relaxed to 3,000 metres, not quite high enough for Bolivia's stadium in the sky.

Maradona has been credited with saying, 'All of us have to play where we were born. Not even God can ban that, and certainly not Blatter. The measure is ridiculous. It's disgraceful. It was approved by people who have never chased a football. It's political.'

As a result, the ban was lifted, allowing the Bolivian national team to recommence playing their home games in La Paz. At the time of writing Bolivia are 12 games into qualification for World Cup 2010. They are winless away, losing 3–0 to Argentina, only to win their return game in La Paz 6–1. Absolutely ridiculous.

In a nutshell, Bolivia only achieves success as a footballing force by the virtue of the fact that the other team can't breathe. For once, maybe Sepp Blatter was talking sense.

Queens Park Rangers has had to move home no less than 20 times, since 1886, and that could soon be 21 if their new money men deliver on their plans for a bigger stadium.

7

And When You're Not Playing Football?

43. A Double for the Animal, and a Lager Tops for the Monkey

If Paul Gascoigne, as Sir Bobby Robson suggested, is as 'daft as a brush', then one man could accurately be charged with being as mad as a whole rainforest full of frogs.

So frequent have been his deviances from the path to righteousness, that I feel it necessary to bestow on him the dubious honour of being the only player to earn his very own 'section of shame'.

Otherwise, the name of Brazilian star Edmundo would continually pop up in countless stories throughout these pages, due to the simple fact that he has been regularly touched by the hand of near insanity. Some of his actions over the years were funny, others were fatal.

While other bad boys could match him on counts of fighting, criminal charges and outspokenness, he stands alone as the only footballer who ever pulled a jersey on in

---

Rangers are officially the most successful league side in the world. They've lifted the top trophy in Scottish football 52 times, and picked up 109 trophies in all, and counting. However, if you include cups not endorsed by UEFA, the title reverts to Irish League side Linfield, who have won over 200.

---

earnest to have been accused of getting a monkey drunk.

A family man at heart, Edmundo wanted to celebrate the first birthday of his cherished son in style, so, in 1999, he did what any loving father would do. He hired an entire circus to perform in his own back garden.

I'm not talking about a Punch and Judy show here, but the whole shebang – elephants, jugglers, clowns, trapeze artists, the lot.

Amongst the travelling carnival was Pedrinho, a monkey of some distinction who had travelled the length and breadth of Brazil without any incident of note. That was, until he met Edmundo.

As the kids played, the adults drank, with the coolest dad in the world revelling in the glory of a party well planned.

Right from the beginning, Edmundo and Pedrinho hit it off famously, aping around and causing trouble. As the monkey business continued, the Brazilian allegedly plied his new friend with copious amounts of beer and whisky, a charge which he later vehemently denied.

His case, however, might have been stronger if a picture hadn't surfaced of him sitting, all glazy eyed and sunburnt, tipping a pint glass down Pedrinho's throat. Animal Rights groups the world over went ballistic, but on close inspection of the offending picture both parties looked by all accounts to be having the time of their lives!

The whole unsavoury saga cemented his nickname as 'The Animal', and was added to a classic list of Edmundo moments.

One such occurrence that has hung around his neck

more than the monkey did, comes with not a single iota of humour.

In 1995, whilst signed to Italian side Fiorentina, he was driving back from a Brazilian nightclub with three women in tow when he crashed head-on into an oncoming car, killing three people.

He was found guilty of road negligence and sentenced to four and a half years in prison. However, after a whole procession of appeals from his lawyers, one of them was eventually upheld. Three others were seriously injured, but Edmundo walked away from the mangled mess with only bruises, which makes sense considering he was driving a truck.

It's these two stories that will live with this man as much as anything he's ever achieved in sport, which includes 12 goals in 36 games for his national side, and successful spells with the likes of Vasco da Gama and Palmeiras, although he never stayed put for long.

Even on the field, he was known to self-combust, earning a reputation for seeing red.

Once, against São Paulo, he lost his head completely. After lunging in with a vicious slide tackle, he proceeded to pick himself off the floor, dust himself down and run towards his opponents' dugout.

> *Reading*'s former players include none other than George Best. Although he never played competitively, he turned out for four 1982 pre-season friendlies before heading to Bournemouth. This spell doesn't appear on most of Best's official lists of clubs.

When he got there he waged war on the substitutes, slapping the first, actually knocking out the second, and kicking his third victim squarely where the sun don't shine.

Asked to explain one of the most random assaults ever witnessed, he claimed they were saying discourteous things about his mother. Ah right, I understand now. Totally acceptable.

It's not just his enemies who need to watch out. On various occasions he's lashed out at his own team-mates, once again allowing passion to cloud any form of human reasoning.

He once accused his fellow Fiorentina player Leonardo of not passing the ball to him for a whole 90 minutes. Whether or not he had grounds for complaint was offset by the fact that the game in question was a pre-season friendly against Atletico Bilbao.

Not one for holding his tongue, in the very same summer he publicly stated that he should have played in the 1998 World Cup finals ahead of Bebeto, saying that he was not only better physically and technically, but was simply 'better than Bebeto'.

During his time in Europe controversy was never far away, including one occasion when he returned to Brazil against the club's wishes so he could party at the Rio Carnival.

More recently, his inability to control a steering wheel came back to haunt him when he knocked a handyman off a ladder. The incident happened as he was leaving the Vasco da Gama training ground, the club for which he still plays.

One minute the innocent party was trying his best to

fix the air-conditioning system, the next he was eating dirt. This time, however, there was no tragic end, with the striker even offering to pick up the medical bills.

As long as the Animal is still breathing, no footballer, repair man or member of the animal kingdom can truly sleep easily in their beds. Edmundo is a one-off, for all the right reasons ... and the wrong.

44. Love Is Blind, Football Is Deaf

I consider my two passions in life to be football and music, but rarely should the two streams cross.

When they do, the most common outcome is so painful that the only way to escape is to burn your radio or cut your ears off. While the latter may seem more drastic, it's the only way to guarantee a lifetime free from heinous crimes against audio committed by some of our most famous footballers.

Flick through the *Guinness Book of Hit Records* and you'll quickly come to realise that singing, if it's not misleading to call it that, should be left to the fans on the terrace.

I'm not talking about novelty records, when a team get together for a laugh and record an FA Cup final anthem or a World Cup song, but about those who genuinely believe that their success on the field can translate to the stage.

In 1987 Glenn Hoddle, future England manager, and Chris Waddle, the Geordie genius, teamed up to release a travesty called 'Diamond Lights'.

Their appearance on *Top of the Pops* rates as one of the most cringe worthy moments since dinosaurs once roamed the earth.

Decked in outfits more suited to a drugs bust scene in *Miami Vice*, hair mulleted and gelled to within an inch of its life, they stood side be side and earnestly pulled sexy faces to such lyrics as 'Standing in the rain, cold electric sky' and 'Darling I love you, I'll always want you'.

Benefiting from their ill-advised assault was Kevin Keegan, whose mortifyingly sickening musical ditties 'It Ain't Easy' and 'Head over Heels in Love' were easily eclipsed by this diabolical double act.

After bewilderingly reaching number 12 in the charts, the Spurs pairing were encouraged to follow it up with a track called 'It's Goodbye', which was a fitting ode to what was soon to become of both their music careers.

While this is the most famous example, many others have tried and failed to make the crossover.

In 2000 Andy Cole proved that being a hitman on the field does not necessarily make you one off it. He failed to chart with a rap record called 'Outstanding', which was an accurate title given that it stands out as the worst footballer's single of all time, bar none. Even Chris and Glenn could probably afford a laugh at Andy's expense. He's a nice guy in real life, but I have to say that Andy's flow was closer to Mr Blobby than Eminem.

There must be something in the water at Old Trafford that encourages their goalscorers to take to the microphone, and it's a little known fact that Carlos Tevez fronts a band called Piola Vago.

> **Rhyl** shares its nickname with Tottenham Hotspur, namely 'the Lilywhites', and remains a part-time club despite its current league success, and the fact that the team has Welsh internationals in their line-up.

A smash hit in his native Argentina with tracks such as 'Lose Your Control', the David Banner look-alike will tell you that it's traditional South American music and not for the Western audience.

Truthfully, after visiting their Myspace, I can confirm that, regardless of its genre, our Carlos has a talent more suitable to an *X Factor* outtakes reel.

Another transatlantic disaster story is delivered by Alexei Lalas, which goes to show that just because you look like a rock star doesn't automatically mean you are one. The crusty veteran, a past player with Perugia and LA Galaxy, is three albums down the line, each one of them as appalling as the last.

His popularity, however, coupled with the fact that millions of people actually have an unforgivable taste in music, has kept his sales respectable, and he's even been known to take it to the live stage, including European dates opening up for Hootie and the Blowfish, which probably made him sound quite good in comparison.

With a dishonourable mention for Dutch legend Johan Cruyff's oompah-oompah single 'Oei Oei Oei, Dat Was Me Weer Een Loei', and a shameful nod to Frenchman Youri Djorkaeff's '*Vivre dans ta lumiére*' I feel I must redress the balance slightly with stories of former footballers who actually had genuine musical talent.

Obviously, Luciano Pavarotti, despite never being a professional, was an above average player, but there was a Real Madrid youth star who went on to shift over 300 million units, releasing nearly 80 albums to date in 14 different languages, and has teamed up with legends such as Willie Nelson, Diana Ross and Stevie Wonder.

While we think of Julio Iglesias as a cotton-suited slick crooner, in his teenage years he was regarded as quite the goalkeeper, with his performances between the sticks earning him a leading role in the club's youth system.

However, an horrific car crash in the early 1960s ended his career in a split second, with doctors claiming that it was a miracle he ever walked again, never mind play football.

Another massive name was once on the books of Brentford, although his switch to music was his own choice, and a good one at that, given that Brentford were playing in the lower divisions and the man in question was Rod Stewart.

Still, none of the above was actually playing football at the time of achieving credibility and success in the music world.

Instead, novelty has ruled the day, from Gazza's 'Fog on the Tyne' to Baddiel and Skinner's legendary 'Three Lions'. I have a personal penchant for the 1970 England squad's 'Back Home' and Scotland's 1982 tongue-in-cheek World Cup classic 'We Have a Dream'. And we can't ridicule any of these songs – not even Arsenal's terrifying 1998 take on Donna Summer's 'Hot Stuff', because they're only intended as a laugh in the first place.

> *St Mirren's* first official floodlit game did not take place until 1956, but they played a night match some 66 years earlier, against Morton in 1890. The clash didn't take place in pitch darkness, however, as the pitch was illuminated by a series of oil lamps.

So, is there just one example of a footballer who took to the stage without a cheap gimmick and left with his reputation intact? Possibly, although he needed the guidance of some true heavyweights.

After a decent start on the 'Anfield Rap', John Barnes brought his hip-hop potential to the most credible football song ever, and it positively flourished.

As far as music goes, there's never been a better-penned football song than England New Order's 'World in Motion', and Digger's rhymes finally brought tuneful honour to a profession shrouded in shame.

Beginning with 'You've got to hold and give, but do it at the right time', and ending with the triumphant 'We ain't no hooligans, this ain't a football song. Three lions on my chest, I know we can't go wrong', Barnes's flow was a virtual tidal wave.

Let's hope this one example does not encourage today's stars to have a serious crack at singing stardom. Just the thought of Ashley Cole doing a straight-faced cover of Tammy Wynette's 'Stand by Your Man' has me reaching for the Stanley knife.

45. There's No Smoke Without Players

People need heroes. The world needs heroes. And to the youth of today, their idol more often than not comes in the form of a world-class athlete.

Unlike in decades gone by, a false image has developed of a star who trains hard, doesn't drink, doesn't cheat on his missus and spends his entire life devoted to winning football matches on your behalf.

With every fresh edition of a tabloid newspaper this perfect vision is dealt a body blow, as a nation gasps and recoils in disgust at sordid tales of two-timing, professional grannies and cocaine-fuelled binges, all serving to shatter our conceptions.

In reality, it is unrealistic to expect any group of males, chosen at random, to behave any differently from the next bunch, which is why football includes its fair share of hoodlums, common criminals and big-mouthed yobs.

The collective vice that all wayward footballers share is that of stupidity, throwing it all away for a few beers, a line of charlie or a quick leg-over, making headlines and knocking our legends off their pedestals.

The key, therefore, is getting away with it, and there's one vice that has been omnipresent in football, but only occasionally gains column inches.

When you think about it, the idea of a professional

footballer smoking is fairly nonsensical, considering how important stamina is to their performance. I know this only too well, as somebody who took up smoking in his early twenties. I went from a box-to-box player to a carton-to-carton holding midfielder.

Delve back into the days of black and white and you'll find countless scrapbooks of photos and footage of players sparking up in the changing room or in the sunken baths, before and after matches.

Some took it a step further, actually appearing in advertisements encouraging their legions of devotees to embrace the nasty habit!

Sir Stanley Matthews, regarded as one of the all-time greats, played at the highest level until he was 50 years old, a feat accredited to his fanatical fitness regime. Matthews, it goes without saying, didn't smoke, but appeared in advertisements in 1954 that tied his 'smooth ball control' into 'the smoothness of Craven A'.

He wasn't the only one who, albeit less aware of the dangers of smoking than we are today, publicly advocated it.

Dixie Dean, Everton's ultimate icon, is another notable poster boy. He promoted Carreras Club, a cheap tab aimed at the working man. Apparently, according to the advertisement, they were 'the cigarettes with the kick in them'.

Back in the day, it seems smoking was no real biggie, with Brazilian icon Socrates openly choking his way through 40-a-day throughout his entire career, which is ironic when you consider he went on to work as a doctor.

Dutch maestro Johan Cruyff learned the hard way – his

heavy-smoking antics helped him on his way to heart surgery in 1991. Since then, he has been an active anti-smoking advocate, including fronting a campaign for the Catalan government during his time at Barcelona.

Returning to the 21st century, you would imagine the problem had all but been extinguished, but dig a little deeper and you'll find a long, long list of footballers who indulge in the odd packet or six.

Of course, some hardly bear referencing, namely Joey Barton and his cigar habit, which took a back seat to the fact that he stubbed it out in Man City team-mate Jamie Tandy's eye.

The crime was also downgraded for Gazza and Teddy Sheringham, who where both pictured puffing away on the infamous 'dentist chair' in the Hong Kong scandal during England's Euro 1996 preparations.

The black-lunged roll-call of regular and occasional puffers is just too long to document.

In 1998 the pro-smoking lobby FOREST actually printed a rather distasteful Fantasy Smokers First XI. There were quite a few of this squad who could have played in midfield or up front, but it technically lines up as a rather peculiar 2–6–2 formation. I suppose smokers can't be choosers.

In goal, the filter tip was Dino Zoff. At the back, a

Scunthorpe United's manager Nigel Adkins used to be their physio, but was promoted to gaffer after the 2006 departure of Brian Laws, which is why the Glanford Park faithful chant, 'Who Needs Mourinho? We've got our physio.'

smoke-screen was provided by Jack Charlton and Frank Leboeuf. The spluttering midfield engine consisted of Socrates and Gerson, with Osvaldo Ardiles and David Ginola wheezing up and down the wings. This left both Bobby Charlton and Robert Prosinecki free to clog up the midfield or support the forward line of Jimmy Greaves and Malcolm MacDonald, who by all accounts were on fire up front. Rather amusingly, FOREST also named Gazza as their sole substitute.

If FOREST had so wished, they could have planned a whole virtual tournament to honour the joys of smoking, albeit, in some cases, occasional. Here's my entirely different starting XI, not using any player named thus far. I've christened them Lungs XI, and they line up in an orthodox 4–3–3 formation.

In goal, it's David James every day of the week, although Fabien Barthez was deemed a serious contender.

In defence, I'm lucky to have Des Walker available for selection. He'll be partnered by Arsenal's William Gallas, lambasted by Arsene Wenger after being spotted falling out of a nightclub with a fag hanging from his gob.

At this stage I would like to announce my player-manager – the colourful Slaven Bilic, who chain-smoked his way through playing stints at West Ham and Everton, continuing to this very day, now as a manager, to put away the butts like there's no tomorrow.

Completing the back line and providing a much-needed hatchet man is Neil 'Razor' Ruddick, who was snapped smoking outside a bar in Liverpool.

In the holding role it has to be Dietmar Hamann, partnered by the most famous modern-day smoker of them all, Zinedine Zidane. Zizou was pictured puffing away on the day of France's World Cup 2006 semi-final against Portugal.

Heavy smoker Frank Rijkaard completes the midfield.

I have quite a team building up, I think you'll agree, but it's the forward line that's truly smokin'! I give you Wayne Rooney, papped recently, poolside in Vegas, merrily making short work of a cancer stick. He'll be joined by a familiar face and occasional smoker Dimitar Berbatov, with the world-class threesome being completed by Italy's Gianluca Vialli, who is rumoured to have sneakily sparked up beside the bench after being substituted in the 1996 World Cup.

That's a lung-busting starting XI, especially when you consider my two substitutes are Maradona and Robin Van Persie.

Finally, one funny story alleges that Peter Crouch, freshly signed by Liverpool and celebrating a big victory, went to spark up a cigarette only for Gary McAllister to slap him on the back of his head, reprimanding him for being so stupid.

That's a crying shame, as Lungs XI could have done with some extra height up front.

Sheffield United was the first club in the world to buy a Chinese team. Chengdu Wuniu were renamed Chengdu Blades in 2006, and you can buy replica jerseys of both sides in their respective club shops.

46. Badges? We Don't Need No Stinking Badges!

In football there are some burning questions that will for ever be debated as long as the world keeps turning.

Did the ball cross the line in the 1966 World Cup final? Why was Ronaldo originally left out of Brazil's 1998 World Cup final side, only to be reinstated at the 11th hour? Was Andriy Shevchenko really spying on Mourinho on Abramovich's behalf? All of these puzzles, however, pale in comparison to the big one, the $64,000 question . . .

Who wrecked the *Blue Peter* garden?

Since 1958 various teams of presenters have been entertaining the nation with their hugely successful charity appeals, the famous *Blue Peter* badge, and, of course, making toys out of toilet rolls at every available opportunity.

The jewel in the crown was, and still is, the *Blue Peter* garden, designed by none other than gardening guru Percy Thrower, God rest his soul. It has always been the epicentre of the show's spirit and soul.

On 21 November 1983 *Blue Peter* was to suffer its darkest hour, when a nation stood united and appalled in equal measure after hoodlums broke into the garden and tore it to shreds. These lowlifes poured fuel oil into the fish pond, broke an ornamental urn (an urn!), smashed a sundial to smithereens and, on their way out, ruined all the flowerbeds.

Then presenters Janet Ellis and Peter Duncan could hardly hold back the tears as they announced to the viewers that, effectively, nothing was sacred these days. Percy Thrower also weighed in, referring to the at-large perpetrators as 'mentally ill'.

But what the heck has football got to do with the *Blue Peter* garden? Read on ...

The myth goes that, as a young whippersnapper growing up in the White City housing estate adjacent to BBC Television Centre, none other than Sir Les Ferdinand – QPR, Spurs, Newcastle and England goal-scoring machine – was part of the Motley Crew who vaulted the wall and desecrated the hallowed ground of the *Blue Peter* garden ... but is it true, or just a tall tale?

The fable arose from a random comment Ferdinand made in an interview. The journalist had worked out that the player had grown up in that area around the same time and, out of the blue, jokingly asked him if he had been involved. Ferdinand simply said no, and the conversation moved on, but from there the rumours started.

Despite their complete lack of foundation, Ferdinand was asked on a regular basis about his alleged involvement, to the point that he started making jokes to ease the boredom of repetition. During the BBC Choice programme called *45 Minutes* in 2000, he went as far as to say he'd helped a few people over the wall, adding, 'I'm not at liberty to say whether Dennis Wise was one of them.' Now Dennis the Menace was in the People's Dock!

The fall-out from these flippant remarks, even 17 years

after the actual event, blew up in Ferdinand's face, with tabloid hacks camping outside his house in a witch-hunt to nail those responsible for the worst crime in children's TV history. Les has since revealed in a *Guardian* interview that one journo thrust pictures of a sobbing Percy Thrower into his face and asked him for a response.

In that same interview, Sir Les said the notion that he had actually torn up the flowerbeds or killed the goldfish was 'ridiculous'.

So, for legal reasons, it must be stated that Sir Les Ferdinand did not wreck the *Blue Peter* garden. Why? Because there is not a single shred of evidence linking either Les or Dennis to the scene of the crime, apart from Ferdinand's light-hearted, ill-advised remarks.

Still, he'll no doubt spend the rest of his life denying it, and fans will spend the rest of their days spreading, as if it were gospel, the story of Les Ferdinand destroying the *Blue Peter* garden. Can he complain? No, he can't. You started it, Les.

47. Balls, Balls and More Balls

L adies and gentlemen, Colin Murray Enterprises brings
you ... the Greatest Misconception In Football ...
'Modern-day players, with their fancy cars and their big
wages, are a disgrace. In my day, this would never have
happened.'

There is one main reason why people wrongly believe
that stars of the past used to walk around with shiny halos,
stopping only to help old people across the street, and that
is because they could get away with their misdemeanours.
The media, you see, did not camp in their back gardens
or pay Page Three lovelies to 'kiss and tell'.

Most of the stories I've been told I can't possibly put in
print, because they were revealed to me in confidence,
mainly by ex-players with whom I have worked over the
past five years or so.

For example, if I was to tell you that Tranmere Rovers
used to charge men a hundred times more in admission
price to their Christmas parties than they did women, Pat

Sheffield Wednesday keeper Kevin Pressman saw red sooner
than any player in British league history. He was sent off 13
seconds into a game against Wolverhampton Wanderers in
2000 for handling outside of the area.

Nevin would do his nut, so I can't possibly betray his trust.

However, we're blessed by the fact that over the years some tales of lady-based debauchery have slipped through the net, confirming beyond all shadow of a doubt that footballers will be footballers, and they always have been.

Unfortunately, we'll never really know what went on in the days before colour telly, but from 1970s onwards, footballers set the bar for today's bad boys, and I'm not just talking about George Best. Allow me to share my favourites with you.

The king of them all has to be Frank Worthington, who has never been backward in coming forward about his debauched exploits. So much so that he had the audacity to name his autobiography *One Hump or Two?*.

An undoubtedly gifted player, he only ever managed eight England caps, and will go down in history, alongside others such as Rodney Marsh, Stan Bowles and Alan Hudson, as somewhat of a missed opportunity.

To this very day he's a hero amongst Bolton Wanderers and Leicester City fans, but his chance to move to the greatest team in the world was directly scuppered by his love of – how can I put this delicately? – the finer things in life.

In 1972 Bill Shankly had successfully negotiated a deal with Huddersfield Town to bring the striker to Anfield, where Worthington would be joining a side who were about to hoover up domestic and international honours at an unprecedented rate. Big Frank even made it to Merseyside itself, before his medical revealed unusually high blood pressure, accredited to his 'life less ordinary'.

Undeterred, Shanks sent the star on holiday to Majorca,

confident that a few days of rest and relaxation would reduce his reading enough to complete the dream move.

Legend has it that, rather than reclining on the beach, Frank Worthington indulged in dalliances with a Miss Great Britain, a well-stacked Belgian and two Swedish bombshells, the upshot being that he registered even higher blood pressure on his return. The move was called off and with it went the player's chance to fill his trophy cabinet. Still, Miss Great Britain, a well-stacked Belgian and two Swedish bombshells. It's *Sophie's Choice*, isn't it?

He wasn't alone in making this particular decade swing. In fact, one manager seemed to have an 'anything you can do . . .' policy when it came to competing in the bad boy stakes.

Malcolm Allison was gaffer at Manchester City, Crystal Palace and Sporting Lisbon, but matched his passion of the game with a love of cigars, champagne and – surprise, surprise – women.

Not only was he married to a *Playboy* bunny, but he once sent his Selhurst Park squad scrambling for their towels when he burst into the dressing room with porn queen Fiona Richmond on his arm. Amongst the naked bodies that day was one Terry Venables.

Add to that an association of sorts with movie star Jane Russell and Profumo affair model Christine Keeler and

---

Shrewsbury Town boasts the only PA system that goes up to 11! Harry Shearer's character, Derek Smalls, wears a replica jersey in the legendary spoof rockumentary *This is Spinal Tap*.

it's not hard to work out why one Man City player, speaking in *FourFourTwo* magazine, dubbed big Mal 'the Male Prostitute'.

At least Allison and Worthington restricted their extra-curricular activities to strangers and pin-ups. Tommy Docherty was sacked from his managerial post at Manchester United for having a fling with a woman called Mary Brown, who just happened to be the wife of the club physio, Laurie Brown. His P45 came days later, and just six months after he had led his side to FA Cup glory.

Less is known about the shenanigans of the late Peter Osgood, who was a key player during a flamboyant era at Chelsea, both on and off the pitch. So much so that he was christened 'the King of Stamford Bridge'.

Various celebrities would be allowed access to the team changing room, with frequent visitors being the actors Steve McQueen and Raquel Welch, the latter of whom took a bit of a shine to our Pete. How do we know this? Well, because one Saturday afternoon she actually walked along the touchline and waved goodbye to him during a game! I bet his head had never felt so swollen.

From here, you probably know every debauched story involving footballers and their unpredictable zippers, although it would be criminal to wrap this up without a quick nod to the great Peter Shilton.

In 1980 Shilts was parked on a dirt track in the Nottingham area, but the only bird watching he was doing was inside his Jaguar.

Her name was Tina and, unfortunately for the goalkeeper, his liaison was rudely interrupted ... by Tina's husband!

Despite the irate man's best efforts, Peter made a diving save to his right, locking himself and his fancy woman inside the car. When the wronged husband phoned the police, Shilton panicked and in his efforts to escape ploughed straight into a lamppost.

Why the big rush? I think the 15-month ban and £350 fine for drink-driving answers that question.

Thankfully, good-natured fans helped Peter Shilton to remember the day by heartily chanting, 'Does your missus, does your missus, does your missus know you're here?'

Call it cheating, dogging, roasting, frolicking, swinging, whatever you like, but it's clear that great footballers and loose women go hand in hand. Always have done, always will.

48. Football's Outsized Baggage

My favourite kids' TV programme as I was growing up was a cartoon called the Raggy Dolls, based around life in a toy factory reject bin.

These dolls had been thrown into the rubbish because they were too tall, too fat, too short or too ugly for public consumption. I can still sing the theme tune word for word. I'm doing it now, you just can't hear me, because this is a book.

Football's only prerequisite for acceptance is talent. It's the only passport you need to fame and fortune, regardless of the circumference of your head or the size of your feet. So, throughout time, there has been a special collection of players who, had they not been good at football, would have been laughed at by people in the street.

Now, I do not wish to pen a cruel piece on 'football freaks', but instead pay tribute to those who have battled against weight, aesthetics and gravity, to beat the odds and make it in the game they love. Just like the Raggy Dolls, they put up with the jibes and the wisecracks, and came out the other side smelling of roses or, in some cases, bacon fat.

Before I begin, this is also not an excuse to vilify Peter Crouch who, despite standing at a giant 6ft 7in, is joined by Aston Villa's Zat Knight, Sunderland's Marton Fulop and his former team-mate at Portsmouth, Asmir Begovic, as the current four tallest Premier League players. All of these names are outgrown by Czech monster striker Jan Koller, who measures up at 6ft 7$\frac{1}{2}$in.

The true Goliath of football, however, is Kristof van Hout, who plays for KV Kortrijk in Belgium and stretches to a cloud-bursting three millimetres shy of 6ft 10in.

Worldwide, Crouchy would be lucky to break the top ten tallest chart, with the strangest addition being Chinese striker Yang Changpeng. Though his compatriots are not usually known for their height, he's sprouted to 6ft 8$\frac{1}{2}$in, but is considered to be still in the growing phase, which is a genuine worry for nearby light aircraft. Yang proves that height is not a byword for genuine talent, as he was sent home after an unsuccessful one-month trial at Bolton Wanderers, mainly because he kept punching holes in the dressing-room roof with his noggin.

Chelsea's Petr Cech is one of the tallest top-flight keepers, standing at 6ft 5in, but comes up positively Jimmy Krankie-like when made to stand beside Croatian Vanja Ivesa, who is 6ft 8$\frac{1}{2}$in.

I could be wrong, but I can't find a 7-foot-tall footballer who has ever played the game at a professional level, probably because they immediately get drafted into careers

---

Southampton's St Mary's stadium, built on an old pagan burial ground, was said to be cursed. After failing to win their first five home games, they brought in a white witch to exorcise the ghouls, and promptly beat Charlton in their very next match.

in basketball, WWE Wrestling and light-bulb changing.

While being tall has its advantages, the obvious being in headers, the other end of the scale proves much harder.

Wee 1980s winger Pat Nevin was originally told at 16 by Celtic that he was too short to make it in the game, before going on to play for Chelsea, Everton and Scotland, to name but three.

Currently, Liverpool's Emiliano Insua, Man City's Shaun Wright-Phillips and Spurs' Aaron Lennon are the leading Premier League pipsqueaks, creeping up to a dwarf-like 5ft 5in, the same size as Diego Maradona and Barcelona's Lionel Messi.

There are smaller ones but not by much. River Plate's Diego Buonanotte is only 5ft 2in, but given that Gary Coleman from *Diff'rent Strokes* managed to reach 4ft 8in, there's never been a sub-5ft adult footballer, unless you include the humourlessly named Giants of the North, a Brazilian senior side made up entirely of dwarves and midgets.

The first of their kind, they play regularly against youth sides in order to even out their disadvantage, and have been known to field players as small as 3ft 7in. None of them, however, has yet impressed enough to warrant a trial in the 'big' leagues.

Moving on from vertical to horizontal, there is only one player, and one alone, who put the 'fat' into football.

During the late 1800s and early part of the 20th century he participated at the highest level for Sheffield United, Chelsea and Bradford City, picking up two FA Cup medals and a league Championship along the way.

He also represented England on one occasion, although

it's not known whether or not they found a cap big enough for him.

So rotund was William Foulke that he was commonly known as 'Fatty', and was said to have ballooned to a gut-busting 25 stone by the end of his career.

It is widely believed, but entirely inaccurate, that the chant 'Who Ate All the Pies?' was invented in his honour.

He did, however, use his bulk to his advantage, the most famous instance of this being at the end of a 1902 FA Cup draw against Southampton. Then a Blade, Fatty was furious that the Saints equaliser had been aloud to stand.

His famous temperament got the better of him shortly after the game, and he wobbled naked from the dressing room and attempted to assault referee Tom Kirkham. Faced with the unique sight of a nude Fatty blubbering towards him like an out of control life-sized sherry trifle, he hid inside a cupboard, while several FA officials desperately hung from the player's every limb in an attempt to contain him.

As club captain at Chelsea, he would sometimes waddle off the field during a match if he thought his own players weren't putting in enough effort, although some felt this was just a cover story, allowing him the chance to get at the half-time sandwiches before the rest of his side.

> **Southend United** is the only team to have played Manchester United and still boast a 100 per cent record against them. They beat them 1–0 in the fourth round of the 2006/07 League Cup, a giant killing which remains their only ever clash with the Red Devils.

The most famous fatty, however, was Micky Quinn, who played for the likes of Newcastle United, Portsmouth and Coventry throughout the 1980s and into the 90s. Nicknamed Sumo, he was once rumoured to have brushed his teeth with mayonnaise.

The Scouser actually appeared on ITV's *Celebrity Fit Club*, starting at 19st 6lb, and going on admirably to shed four stone.

The problem with weight is that very few players ever recorded their exact size during their playing days. Quinn, however, always took fans' heckling with a real sense of humour. During one match an abusive West Ham fan threw a pie at him. Micky not only caught it but proceeded to eat it during the game.

The most talented lardy of them all is Hungarian legend Ferenc Puskas, who weighed in, as part of the Mighty Magyars, with almost one goal per international match, bagging 84 in 85 caps. At club level, he was just as lethal, hammering home 514 goals in 529 games for Spanish and Hungarian sides.

After a surge of big boys like Jan Molby, Neil Ruddock, Neville Southall and John Hartson, it seemed that the electric pace of 21st-century football had rendered the portly players extinct, but that hasn't stopped Sunderland's Andy Reid and, of course, the infamous Brazilian Ronaldo, from carrying around a spare tyre under their jerseys. As my mother says, there's nothing wrong with a healthy appetite.

So, we've done the tallest, smallest and fattest, which leaves us with the ugliest. Not being an oil painting myself, I am uncomfortable with personally identifying those who may have fallen out of the ugly tree and hit most branches on the way down.

Instead, let me give you a light-hearted XI, featuring players who may not have been graced with classic good looks. I've employed an unorthodox 3–4–3 formation.

In the nets, it has to be Steve Ogrizovic, the Coventry City legend who was barely fit to model socks.

Marshalling the back line is former hatchet man Trifon Ivanov, known to his friends and enemies alike as 'the Bulgarian Wolf', due to his unkempt mullet and beard. The caveman cut of ex-Arsenal idol Martin Keown will help him out, with Bolton's Andy O'Brien completing a defence that could scare the living daylights out of any striker without having to make a single tackle.

Our midfield linchpin and captain is former Manchester United youngster, now playing with MK Dons, Luke Chadwick, but he faces stiff competition for the armband from the obtusely framed Peter Beardsley, chipmunk impersonator Ronaldinho and the toothy-grinned Nobby Styles.

Up front I've gone for the less fashionable trio of cone-headed Robbie Earnshaw, Dirk Kuyt and John Merrick's cousin Ian Dowie, although I have Wayne Rooney and Franck Ribery ready to replace them should they fail to deliver. That decision will be made by my manager, and Gollum's stunt double, David Moyes.

Thankfully, football is not a fashion contest, nor is it judged on ideal weight, height and beauty. It truly is a game for all shapes and sizes.

8

What Could Have Been

49. Regrets, They've Had a Few

They say it's better to have loved and lost, than never to have loved at all, but I'm not sure the nearly men of football would entirely agree.

The fine line between glory and failure is epitomised by a small group of players who have missed out on what would have been the highlight of their career after one rush of blood to the head.

Some have played the villain, others have been hailed as heroes, but all of them have felt the crushing pain of having to sit on the sidelines while their team-mates lived the dream.

In 2002, during the World Cup semi-final, South Korea's Lee Chun-Soo was cutting a hole through Germany's defence all on his own. As his marauding run threatened the edge of the opposition penalty area, and the Germans' very tournament existence, Michael Ballack cynically chopped him to the ground.

The resulting yellow card ruled the midfield dynamo

> **Stockport County** is one of only four English clubs owned by the fans, following the model of the mighty Barcelona. The others are Brentford, Exeter and Notts County, with Stockport being the highest placed.

out of the final, yet four minutes after the booking, Ballack popped up to score the only goal of the game.

Although they would eventually lose to Brazil, the Chelsea player had thrown away his opportunity to take centre stage in the greatest show on earth.

Back home, he was regarded as some sort of superman, with boss Rudi Voller saying, 'He knew he would miss the final but he still committed a tactical foul that was absolutely necessary. If he had not done that, they might have scored. It was a sacrifice for his country and the whole of Germany will applaud him.' And they did.

While Michael had a perverse cloak of adoration to shield the hurt, Alessandro Costacurta could have been forgiven for hanging his boots up altogether in 1994 after a double whammy meant he missed not one, but two champagne moments.

Firstly, he was suspended for AC Milan's emphatic 4–0 annihilation of Barcelona in the Champions League final, and then he was banished from the World Cup final that very summer for Italy, after picking up too many cautions in the earlier rounds, although his country lost out to Brazil on penalties.

At least Paul Gascoigne's famous semi-final tears of 1990 didn't carry over into the following week, with England failing to progress to the final.

Instead, that unwelcome honour was left to Argentina's Claudio Caniggia, who began his campaign by being literally battered by Cameroon, whose defence did their best to decapitate him on their way to a shock 1–0 win in the opening game.

The lank-haired centre-forward went on to score a

second-round goal to dispose of Brazil, and then banged in a decisive equaliser in the semi-final against Italy.

Late in that game, however, he mysteriously handled the ball for little or no reason and was forced to sit out the big match against West Germany. Without their star striker, they lost 1–0, in what may have been the least enjoyable World Cup final of all time.

A serious blow for France's Laurent Blanc should also be acknowledged. He missed out on his side's home soil glory in 1998, after being sent off in the semi-final against Croatia for putting his hand in the face of Slaven Bilic, who reacted as though Blanc had shot him at point-blank range. It was a ridiculous punishment, but that was little comfort to the defender as he took his place with the fans.

Away from the international stage, the best two examples of regretful footballers would have to be Roy Keane and Paul Scholes, who both sat out Manchester United's famous European turnaround against Bayern Munich.

After inspiring the Red Devils to a thrilling semi-final win against Juventus, a foul on Zinedine Zidane saw Keano join Scholesy on the suspended list.

Nine years later Scholes would find redemption, playing in United's penalty shoot-out victory against Chelsea, but Keane would never come any closer to the biggest club stage on the planet.

Stoke City, in 1863, was not only founded by Henry Almond, but he also holds the honour of being their first ever captain and their first ever goalscorer.

He would later describe watching from the stands at the Nou Camp in 1999 as 'just about the worst experience I'd had in football', going on to use phrases such as 'like a spare part' and 'utterly redundant'.

One player turned to the High Court in a bid to reverse his suspension.

Steve Foster was captain of the Brighton side who, despite being rooted to the bottom of Division One, made it all the way to Wembley in 1983.

His day in the dock, after picking up a final ban, failed to change the course of history, but he was instead saved by a 2–2 scoreline, meaning that he did, in the end, get to represent his club in the FA Cup final replay, albeit a 4–0 drubbing by Manchester United.

Others, such as Denis Irwin in 1999 and Sol Campbell in 2003, missed FA Cup final wins, but this would be tempered by other red-letter days in their careers.

The same could be said of Spurs' most faithful servant, Steve Perryman, who has made more appearances for the club than any other player in their history. He would taste success as captain, but refused to lift the UEFA Cup in 1984 after being banned for the final, such was his feeling of redundancy.

50. I've Started So I'll Not Finish

Sometimes, as a football fan, the pain of watching from the stands is so excruciating that you inwardly pray for divine intervention.

It may be that your team is being hammered, or maybe you're hanging on to a vital lead, but either way you just want the suffering to end.

The most common source of assistance comes not from the hand of God but from the local electricity company, as floodlight failure plunges a stadium into welcome darkness and gracefully offers up a break from the torment.

Lights going out, however, is exceedingly boring. Throughout history many a game has been abandoned for reasons above and beyond the realms of likelihood, in one instance resulting in a match that technically lasted for 24 days.

Real Madrid were locked at 1–1 with Real Sociedad in

Sunderland attracts the fifth highest average attendance in the Premier League, yet its fans manage to sing louder than any other home support. Readings taken throughout the 2007/08 season showed their highest volume calculated at 129.2 decibels, a league best.

2004, when a bomb scare forced local police to evacuate every last person – players, fans, mascots, tapas sellers – from the Bernabeu. That's around 81,000 people, who all fell foul to what turned out to be a hoax.

Given that 88 minutes had been played, you'd expect officials to declare the game a draw but, then again, that would be far too sensible.

Instead, over three weeks later, the exact same teams returned to the field of play to complete the two minutes and 40 seconds remaining on the clock, which turned into eight, thanks to four minutes of injury time and two substitutions by the home team. In the dying moments, 20,000 *über*-fans watched Zinedine Zidane slot home a penalty to give Real maximum points.

All credit to the Madrid manager for keeping the players focused right until the last minute; or should I say managers, given that during the hiatus Mariano Garcia Remon had been replaced by Vanderlei Luxemburgo.

There was no chance of a rematch between Sheffield United and West Bromwich Albion in 2002, when the since named 'Battle of Bramall Lane' had to be abandoned because the home team didn't have enough players on the field to continue. Simon Tracey, Patrick Suffo and Georges Santos had all seen red, and Michael Brown and Rob Ullathorne had been taken off through injury. All three substitutions had taken place in various reshuffles, so the referee called a halt eight minutes from time because the rules state that both teams must have a minimum of seven players on the pitch. West Brom did not have to return to play out the remainder of the match though, which would have been pointless given that they were winning 3–0.

Sometimes matches don't even start because of circumstances beyond the clubs' control.

In 1999 Torquay United's League Cup clash with Portsmouth was scuppered by a solar eclipse! While it didn't actually affect playing conditions, it did attract coach loads of tourists to Devon, all eager for a closer look at one of nature's true wonders. This left local bobbies short-handed and because there was not enough manpower to police the game at Plainmoor Ground safely, the tie was postponed.

Outside influences also did for Bristol City versus Brentford in 2000, although this time it was due to the marshalling of protests and blockades arising from the fuel crisis.

Most of the time, however, it's those on the pitch who conspire to spoil a full 90 minutes, and on one occasion it was positively shameful.

In a World Cup qualifier in 1989 Brazil were beating Chile 1–0 with 20 minutes remaining in Rio. It was then that Chilean keeper Roberto Rojas collapsed to the ground, writhing in pain whilst clutching his bleeding face.

Swansea City's favourite son, John Charles, was such a nice man that he was nicknamed 'the Gentle Giant'. He was never booked nor sent off in his entire career. At Juventus, fans also nicknamed him 'Il Gigante Buono' – translation not required.

It appeared that a flare had been thrown from the terraces and had struck the hapless goalie in the face. His team-mates showed their solidarity by storming off the field of play, never to return. You can't blame them really. Not, that is, until you see the TV replay.

The flare never struck Rojas, instead landing quite some distance away, but that didn't stop him falling over as if he'd just been taken out by a crack sniper. Whilst on the deck, this creature cut his face with a razor blade he'd hidden inside his glove.

Mercifully, FIFA not only awarded Brazil a 2–0 win, but they prohibited Chile from even trying to qualify for the 1990 and 1994 World Cups. Rojas was banned for life, but the penalty was lifted on appeal in 2001, which is a real shame.

Outside the big leagues, there are a few classic abandonment anecdotes from Sunday League football, including a ding-dong between Royston Village and Mosborough in 2008, which was called off after 80 minutes in the aftermath of the return to the field of an aggrieved player allegedly armed with a golf club and a machete. The Royston madman not only went for the ref, but chased opposition players, which prompted one onlooker to say, 'Having been involved in football for years, I haven't ever seen anything like that. It was a great game ruined by an idiot.'

It's not always the players' fault though, and in one case the 'idiot' was actually the referee. Peterborough North End's tie against Royal Mail AYL came to an abrupt end when Andy Wain threw down his whistle and proceeded to square up to a loud-mouthed goalkeeper, who had vociferously questioned his decisions throughout the game.

After coming to his senses, he took the unprecedented step of sending himself off and, with no qualified replacement available, the players were forced to take an early bath.

While all of the above make for a humorous read, there is no place in football for such farce. It's wholly frustrating when something unexpectedly stops just when it's reaching a climax … I suppose, the most important thing to remember is

---

Swindon Town defender John Trollope played more league games with one club than any other in history. He turned out 889 times, for two decades, between 1960 and 1980.

51. They Have Their Knockers, But ...

When my friend recently took over as manager of an amateur ladies' football team in London, the first thing he did was seek sponsorship.

Only too keen to help out, I opted to finance the equipment of an unbearably cute Italian striker. It's this type of sporting sexism that makes me sick to the stomach. Women's football in the 21st century continues to grow in popularity and credibility, and has come a long way since the English Football Association banned its existence in 1921.

However, things tend to become a little prickly when the fairer sex crosses into a man's world. Whether it's as manager, player or official, most males of the species don't like their football to contain any breasts, or its participants to carry a make-up bag along with their holdall.

The 21st century has seen a blurring of gender lines, if only in some small ways. Just recently, Donna Powell became the first female ever to take charge of a semi-professional or professional club in English football.

She achieved this not through an interview process or various coaching badges, but by winning a competition.

Donna is the turnstile operator at Fisher Athletic and, after raising £500 for the club, she was handed the reins for just one game, as winner of their 'Boss for a Day' scheme. Fisher, in the Blue Square South, were on a run of 11 straight losses, and Eastleigh's 2–1 win, with Donna in charge, made it 12.

Given the circumstances, I think they should have given her a couple more games, as Eastleigh are a top-five club, but her admirable attempts fell on deaf ears.

Eastleigh's director of football, David Malone, was quick to speak out, saying, 'I'm not particularly happy about it, simply because we've got to concentrate our minds on getting three points from the game. I think what they've done is unprofessional.' Technically, he's not being sexist. Raffling off your manager's position is a bit of a cheap, if not ingenious, trick. Oh no, he left the sexism to the Eastleigh fans, who made their feelings heard at the top of their manly little voices.

Powell commented, 'They kept singing a song about the fact I should have been left in the kitchen making cups of tea.'

Ian Baird, her opposite number on the day, disappeared at the final whistle, with no handshakes taking place. Let's hope Manchester United don't name Caroline Ahern as Sir Alex Ferguson's replacement, or there'll be rioting on the streets of Salford.

The greatest strides in equality have been made in the field of officiating, with recent figures showing that just

Technogroup Welshpool Town suffered their worst defeat in 1997, losing 8–0 to Barry Town, only to inflict the exact same score line on Cemaes Bay in 1998, a more welcomed club record.

under 20 per cent of all FIFA-registered referees and assistants have the ability to give birth, if not to read maps.

Wendy Toms ran the line at the 2000 League Cup final, after making a name for herself in black.

Although her big day out went well, only months previously she had been barracked by then Coventry manager Gordon Strachan, who pointed the finger squarely at her more shapely figure, after his side's 4–3 defeat to Leeds United.

He said, 'We are getting PC decisions about promoting ladies. It does not matter if they are ladies, men or Alsatian dogs. If they are not good enough to run the line they should not get the job. Saturday's was the worst assistant refereeing decision I have seen this season by far and I've said that in my report. The fourth Leeds goal was offside by at least four yards and there were numerous other bad decisions in the game. My message is don't be politically correct and promote people just for the sake of it.'

The ginger Scotsman had a point. We see bad decisions every week, and none of them has any correlation with what's hidden between the official's legs.

Mike Newell, on the other hand, was more candid in his comments on assistant referee Amy Rayner, after his Luton Town side were denied an admittedly blatant penalty against QPR.

His opening gambit is now the stuff of legend . . .

'She shouldn't be here. I know that sounds sexist but I am sexist.'

Just in case he hadn't made himself clear . . .

'This is not park football, so what are women doing

here? It is tokenism – for the politically correct idiots. We have a problem in this country with political correctness and bringing women into the game is not the way to improve refereeing and officialdom. It is absolutely beyond belief.'

Got that? No? Okay . . .

'When do we reach a stage when all officials are women? Because then we are in trouble. It is bad enough with the incapable referees and linesmen we have but if you start bringing in women, you have big problems.'

Fortunately, in football, fines don't discriminate on the grounds of gender, and Newell coughed up nearly £100 for every outspoken word; £6,500 in total.

Personally, I don't feel that the sex of a referee or manager has any bearing on ability, but the waters muddy slightly on the issue of players. Sure, the after-match showers would be a much more eventful place, but should men and women be allowed to play in the same team?

In 2003 it nearly happened for the first time, although the motives behind the move are questionable.

Perugia's president Luciano Gaucci is never one to miss an opportunity for publicity, once trying to sign Libyan footballer Saadi Gaddafi, who would have made the

---

Tottenham Hotspur is the only non-league side ever to win the FA Cup, achieving this amazing feat in 1901. A Spurs official's other half added a feminine touch by tying ribbons to the trophy's handles, a process that's been repeated ever since.

fathers and sons' match a real fiery affair, given that his dad's first name is Colonel.

In 2003 he publicly declared his wish to acquire the services of Swedish pair Hanna Ljungberg and Victoria Svensson, before pursuing German Female World Player of the Year Birgit Prinz. Unsuccessful on both counts, he might have fared better had he thought a little bit more about his sales pitch.

In reference to Prinz, he allegedly declared, without a hint of irony, 'She is very beautiful, and has a great figure. I can assure you that as a player, she's very good.'

When one club did show more reverence, they still hit a brick wall. Mexico's Maribel Dominguez, at her peak in 2004, was one hell of a player.

Such was her form that a Second Division side in her home country, Celaya, broke with tradition and offered her a deserved two-year deal, which she duly signed. FIFA, however, stepped in, forbidding the transfer and, in doing so, drew a clear line between the footballing genders.

Now, I could tell you my opinion on the matter, but I have a mother, two sisters and, hopefully, by the time this book hits the shelves, a girlfriend. So, I'm just going to sit this one out.

I will, however, remind you of the USA's Brandi Chastain, who scored the winning goal at the 1999 World Cup final, then proceeded to rip off her jersey in celebration. At that precise glorious topless moment, women's football showed it can entertain and thrill on a world stage, all by itself.

52. Referee! Are You Blind?
Westlake Clearly Dived!

It's the 1982 World Cup final and Italy are lining up against Brazil. John Motson is assessing the Azzurri's line-up.

'So many greats on the pitch. Rossi should prove the main threat up front, Tardelli is also vital, but let's not forget the man in goal . . . Luciano Pavarotti. Extraordinary.' Now, you may find the fantasy image of the late, great, overweight opera singer diving spectacularly to keep out a stinging drive from Zico quite preposterous but, without motherly intervention, this could have been a reality.

If so, then Pav's lungs would have been reserved not for rousing renditions of 'Nessun Dorma', but for bellowing at his back four for not holding the line correctly.

As a young teenager, his mum persuaded him to choose music over football, despite the fact that he had the gift of the glove, not to mention outfield ability as a winger.

Tranmere Rovers have their very own 'public holiday'. On 27 January, they celebrate Saint Yates' Day, named after defender Steve Yates, who scored two goals in their historic 3–0 FA Cup drubbing of rivals Everton at Goodison Park in 2000/01.

He actually had trials at Modena, at the age of 12, opting for the tuxedo over the home kit.

I am afraid this proves that talent is not evenly distributed throughout humankind, and there are many football players, past and present, who were front of the queue when God, Buddha, Mohammed or Richard Dawkins was handing out sporting prowess.

Let's warm up a little first, starting with Andy Goram, the ex-Rangers and Manchester United goalie. He not only played international football for Scotland, but also represented his country at cricket, which makes sense given his ability to catch a ball.

In a role reversal, Ian Botham played football for Scunthorpe United, making 14 appearances on a match-by-match basis in the early 1980s.

England's greatest cricketing all-rounder originally trained with the club during the winter to keep fit, but so impressive were his ball skills that he ended up being drafted into the first team.

This has given birth to one of the greatest pub quiz posers of all time . . .

QUESTION: Which three former England captains played football for Scunthorpe?
ANSWER: Kevin Keegan, Ray Clemence and Ian Botham.

However, even Beefy can't hold a candle to my favourite example of a crossover sportsman who could have conquered the world in an entirely different set of stadiums.

One current football player was such a good youth

cricketer that he outshone and overshadowed none other than Andrew Flintoff.

Both represented the Lancashire Under-13 side and Freddie commented in his recent autobiography, 'I didn't get much of an opportunity because Phil would bowl teams out.'

The Phil he refers to goes by the second name of Neville. The ex-England and Manchester United man, and current Everton stalwart, was not only outstanding with the ball but also with the bat.

In fact, Flintoff s father, Colin, made a remarkable comment in an interview for the *Telegraph*. He said, 'If I'd had to put money on one schoolboy playing cricket for England at that time, it would have been Phil Neville. Phil was left-handed, and was the best schoolboy batsman I have ever seen.'

However, he chose the ball at his feet rather than in his hands. One true legend decided to just do both, in quite breathtaking fashion.

Denis Compton not only won the 1947/48 league title and 1950 FA Cup with Arsenal, but he also liked to dabble at the crease. He played 78 international tests, with a 50-plus average, putting him up there with the best English cricketers of all time. While Neville had the potential to be a two-sport great, Compton actually realised that improbable dream.

> ***Walsall*** has never been in England's top flight, and hasn't even come close since the 1898/99 season, when the club finished sixth in Division Two.

Now, before you become sick with envy, take solace in the fact that England's 1966 World Cup hero Sir Geoff Hurst made one, and one only, County Championship appearance for Essex in 1962 and was bowled for a duck. Loser!

Also, allow yourself to snigger at the fact that Daley Thompson, a double Olympic gold medal-winning decathlete, couldn't make his talents stretch to football, despite his best efforts. His highlight came when he made one appearance for Mansfield Town in a bottom tier league game against Cardiff City. I say appearance, but he was an unused substitute. Back to the pole vault with you, Daley, my old son.

There are other decent two-sport professionals, but only one that defies belief, and it happened only because of an off-the-cuff comment and an audacious dare.

Ian Westlake, then at Ipswich Town, was lounging around with his team-mates watching the 2004 Athens Olympics, and witnessed Karen Pickering's superhuman fourth appearance at the games in the 50m freestyle.

Although she never quite managed an Olympic podium finish, she boasted quite a medal haul at World, European and Commonwealth levels, a feat that earned her an MBE for her services to sport.

As the players were swept away in a wave of patriotism, Westlake calmly stated, 'I could swim faster.' The seed was sown.

After much cajoling by his pals, eventually Ian and Karen both stood side by side at a swimming pool for what has to be one of the oddest match-ups in the history of sport.

Pickering, obviously, was a huge favourite. Bookmakers, tongue planted firmly in cheek, announced odds of 6 to 1 on for the amphibious athlete, and 7 to 2 for Westlake.

Despite having represented England at junior level at water polo, it appeared that the midfielder was totally out of his depth.

His fellow players crowded the banks of the swimming baths, eager to see their bragging pal get taught a harsh lesson, but instead he bombed his way to an emphatic victory, touching at 25.21 seconds, a massive 0.53 seconds faster than his Olympic counterpart.

James Beattie was also no fish out of water, with only a shoulder injury halting his young swimming career. At the time, he was ranked number 2 in the country.

It makes you sick, doesn't it? While the vast majority of us struggle to stay facing the right way up on a five-a-side pitch, others are truly blessed with ability.

Still, I can balance up to 32 coins on my elbow, catching them in the palm of my hand in one quick flash. I'd like to see Phil Neville try that.

Watford's famous fan Elton John really can't say goodbye. After two stints as chairman, he still holds shares and returned in 2005 to play a concert at Vicarage Road with all profits going directly to the club.

53. It's a Chicken and Egg Situation

When I was in primary school, my class were only beaten twice during break and lunchtime in a whole year.

I was eight at the time, and there were three classes in all, but we were head and shoulders above the competition, mainly due to one player called Johnny who, almost every day, replicated Maradona's wonder goal against England in 1986, despite having just wolfed down a plate of chips and a bowl of pink custard. He remains to this day one of my favourite footballers of all time, but I'm damned if I can remember his surname.

On the last day of term, we pulled on our white kit for the annual Primary 5 Tournament. We'd already decided who would lift the trophy; we'd choreographed individual goal celebrations and agreed which young girlies we would romance as heroes of the playground.

What actually transpired was a 1–1 draw and a 2–1 defeat, the fatal goal coming off the back of a blatant handball by a ginger kid called Neil, I think.

To this day, I've never forgiven that PE teacher turned referee, but deep in my heart I know it was complacency that cost us the silverware.

Counting your chickens before they hatch is a rare sight in football. Managers live by the 'one game at a time' philosophy, but our kids' side didn't have Brian Clough to guide us. Instead, we spent the morning of our big games swapping Panini football stickers.

In 1998, when Manchester United were 11 points clear of Arsenal with just ten games left, you never once heard Sir Alex Ferguson claim that his side were home and hosed. He's too much of a professional, a master of his art, to make such a blunder. Instead, he left that job to the fans.

United fanatic and bookmaker Fred Done cracked open the champagne at the beginning of March, and at the same time ordered that all bets on a United title should be paid out in full. It doesn't need Sue Barker to tell you 'what happened next'. As Arsenal hauled back the deficit and lifted the trophy, poor old Fred was left to cough up again, only this time on wagers received on the Gunners. His premature party cost him a crushing £500,000.

I'm sure Arsenal fans had a good laugh at this, but they've been on the receiving end as well, when in 1991 it was revealed that they'd already been measured up for their FA Cup final suits, *before* their semi-final with Tottenham Hotspur.

Paul Gascoigne masterminded a 3–1 Spurs win, scoring one of the greatest free kicks of all time, and used his post-match interview to rub it into his rash rivals,

West Bromwich Albion is top of the tree in the most unlikely of categories. Standing at 552 feet above sea level their home stadium, the Hawthorns, has the highest altitude of any English league club.

enthusing, 'I'm off to get my suit measured!' Egg . . .
face . . .

We have to leave British football for the cruellest case
of chicken counting, which took place in Germany on the
very last day of the 2000/01 season.

Bayern Munich had every right to be cautious. Even
with a three-point advantage over Schalke, they were
aware of their inferior goal difference, so they headed to
Hamburg knowing what was required.

Schalke, on the other hand, knew they had to beat the
unfancied Unterhaching at home, which they finally did
in style, although they went two goals down before
thumping home five in reply, the final score being 5–3.

As the final whistle sounded, dream news arrived from
elsewhere. A 90th-minute bullet header from Sergej
Barbarez had given Hamburg a one-goal lead, and handed
Schalke the league title.

Fans flooded the pitch, players broke down in tears of
joy, but what they didn't know was that the Bayern match
had kicked off late, something that became apparent when
live coverage of said game was flashed up on the big screen
inside the Schalke stadium.

Suddenly, the celebrations stopped, a deathly silence
fell on Gelsenkirchen, and they watched in disbelief as
almost immediately Patrik Andersson slammed home an
equaliser with virtually the last kick of the game, handing
Bayern Munich the title by one solitary point.

Schalke's hasty merriment earned them the unwanted
nickname of '*Der Vier-Minuten-Meister*', which roughly
translates as 'The Four-Minute Champions'. Cluck cluck.

Elsewhere in this book I've dealt with England's shock

1970 World Cup quarter-final 3–2 defeat to West Germany. Undoubtedly, Gordon Banks's mystery illness was the headline story, but it should be noted that, at 2–1 up with 20 minutes left, Sir Alf Ramsey decided to withdraw Bobby Charlton, possibly to keep him fresh for the semi-final. Oh dear.

Back at Old Trafford, during the 1989/90 season it was a man in a suit who entered the coop a little too early.

Property mogul Michael Knighton, not to be confused with David Hasselhoff's character from *Knight Rider*, agreed a £20m takeover of the club. He was introduced to the crowd before an Arsenal game. He even did some keepy-uppys in the centre circle. He waved to the masses, blew loving kisses to the Stretford End, then settled back to watch his newly acquired venture spank their southern visitors 4–1.

What emerged after full time was nothing short of mind-boggling. Knighton didn't have enough money to buy the club, and the deal fell through, leaving himself, the fans and the club with red faces.

There is only one certainty in football and that's the referee's final whistle. It's then, and only then, we can break out the bubbly. Andy Gray's commentary as Hernan Crespo slotted home AC Milan's third in the 44th minute

---

***West Ham United*'s** nickname 'The Irons' has a particular relevance to one celebrity fan. Iron Maiden bassist Steve Harris has a West Ham sticker on his bass guitar and actually played youth football for the side. Rock 'n' roll.

of the 2005 Champions League final against Liverpool, is testimony to that.

'Game . . . well and truly . . . over.'

Wigan Athletic, after being refused election to the football league on 34 separate instances, applied to join the Scottish Second Division in 1972. They were turned down on the grounds that they were, well, from Wigan.

54. The Greatest Never Player

Some footballers are destined for immortality, while others have it cruelly taken away from them.

Sit around in any pub in the world and listen to punters verbally compiling their all-time a-lists, and the likes of Pele, Maradona and Best will pop up again and again. Rightfully so.

Originally, I intended to assemble a starting XI of players who were robbed of reaching their full potential, but research brought me to the conclusion that one name stands head and shoulders above any other human being, so it's here we honour the greatest player that never was.

The almost royal roll-call of established names who have gone on record to state that this footballer was quite simply the most gifted of all time is truly staggering and unavoidably moving at the same time.

Duncan Edwards was born in Dudley, England, on 1 October 1936. He made his debut for Manchester United when he was 16 years and 185 days old, and

Wolverhampton Wanderers' match against Newcastle United in 1973 brought a whole new meaning to the phrase 'sibling rivalry'. Kenny Hibbitt scored the opening goal, only for his brother Terry Hibbitt to bang in an equaliser.

quickly became the heartbeat of a side who won two league titles in 1955/56 and 1956/57. He would reach 177 appearances.

His uniqueness made him the youngest player to earn an England cap in the 20th century, coming on against Scotland in 1955, when he was 18 years and 183 days old. He would represent his country 18 times.

The Busby Babe spent 15 days battling for his life, following the Munich air disaster on 21 February 1958. Duncan Edwards died when he was 21 years and 158 days old.

In his final moments, it is said that he remarked to assistant manager Jimmy Murphy, 'What time is the kick-off against Wolves, Jimmy? I mustn't miss that match.'

Duncan Edwards was an old-fashioned right-winger, but could just as easily slot in as a centre-back or a centre-forward when asked, and could do the job better than almost any footballer ever to walk the planet.

Nowhere in the annals of football history, random or otherwise, can I find one word to counter the emphatic claim that he was a sporting phenomenon. Anyone who played with him was humbled by it, and anyone who played against him was simply terrified. He was almost unplayable, close to unstoppable, yet consummately graceful and unassuming.

The aforementioned Murphy, then manager of Wales, was giving his international players a pre-match team talk before an England clash. A master of preparation, he went through every single opposition player, detailing their strengths and weaknesses. When he finished, one of his team, Reg Davies, remarked that he'd failed to mention Duncan.

Murphy simply gazed at him and spat, 'There is nothing to say that would help us. Just keep out of his way, son.'

In future years Jimmy went on to say, 'When I hear Muhammad Ali proclaim "I am the greatest" I have to smile. You see, the greatest of them all was an English footballer named Duncan Edwards.

'If I shut my eyes I can see him now. Those pants hitched up, the wild leaps of boyish enthusiasm as he came out of the tunnel, the tremendous power of his tackle, the immense power on the ball.'

It's worth pausing to remember that we are talking about a teenager here who had many years to go before reaching his peak. Let us not forget the company he was keeping in that Manchester United side at the time, unarguably one of the best club sides that ever graced a football pitch, yet he was the star.

Just ask Sir Bobby Charlton, who not only played with Edwards, but also did his National Service with him.

'I totally believe he was the best player I ever saw or am likely to see. He was the only person who made me feel inferior. I was never going to be as good as him.' Charlton

Wycombe Wanderers players adopted a 5ft wooden Comanche after winning away to Lincoln City in the last game of the 1999/2000 season. The lucky charm even appeared in a subsequent team photo but disappeared some years later. A Facebook group now exists, demanding its return to Adams Park.

is on record, countless times, repeating these claims and adding to them. It's not only gushing, but conclusive.

'Duncan Edwards has always been in my mind as the best player I ever played with or against. Physically, he was enormous. He was strong and had a fantastic football brain. His ability was complete – right foot, left foot, long passing, short passing. He did everything instinctively. Without question he would have played in the 1966 World Cup and been England captain.'

It seems he may be the only footballer who puts paid to the idea that nobody's perfect. Pele had his superstitious dips in form; Maradona had his air rifles and his drugs; Best had his drinking, womanising and gambling; but Sir Matt Busby himself reckons Duncan Edwards was flawless.

'We used to look at players in training to see if we might have to get them to concentrate on their kicking, perhaps, or their heading, or ball control. We looked at Duncan, right at the start, and gave up trying to spot flaws in his game.'

When Sir Matt says 'right at the start', he is referring to a 15-year-old kid. A child who, before maturity, was bordering on invincible.

There are others who lost their life before fulfilling their football potential. Scotland and Spurs star John White springs to mind. He picked up countless medals and played in every game of Tottenham's 1960/61 Double-winning side, but lost his life in a bizarre incident, being hit by lightning during a round of golf.

Still, the game of football has never quite lost as much as it did the day full time was blown on Duncan Edwards.

Sir Bobby Charlton summed it up when he emotionally stated, 'Today he would be priceless . . . he was just sensational. And he was such a lovely person, a rough diamond, always happy, always wanting to talk about football. Even after the crash he showed he was as hard as nails. He fought his injuries for a fortnight before he actually died. No one else would have fought for so long.'

The next time you raise a glass to the greats, make sure one toast is reserved for Duncan Edwards, the greatest player that never was.

Yeovil Town holds the record for the highest FA Cup attendance involving a non-league club, and it will probably never be beaten. In 1948, when they were humped 8–0 by Manchester United, 81,565 crammed into Maine Road to watch the demolition.